NEW ZEALAND NATIVE PLANTS FOR YOUR GARDEN

JULIAN MATTHEWS
Drawings by Dael Foy

VIKING PACIFIC

Also by Julian Matthews:

A.A. Trees in New Zealand (1983)
Creative Home Landscaping in New Zealand (1984, 1987)
The New Zealander's Garden (1985)
The New Zealand Garden Book (1986)
Landscaping Ideas for New Zealand Gardens (1986)

VIKING PACIFIC
Penguin Books (NZ) Ltd, 182–190 Wairau Road,
Auckland 10, New Zealand
Penguin Books, Ltd, 27 Wrights Lane, London W8 5TZ,
England
Penguin USA, 375 Hudson Street, New York, NY 10014
United States
Penguin Books Australia Ltd, 487 Maroondah Highway,
Ringwood, Australia 3134
Penguin Books Canada Ltd, 10 Alcorn Avenue, Toronto,
Ontario, Canada M4V 1E4
Penguin Books Ltd, Registered Offices: Harmondsworth,
Middlesex, England

First published by Pacific Publishers 1987
10 9 8 7 6 5 4 3 2 1
Copyright © Julian Matthews 1987

The moral right of the author has been asserted.

Printed in Hong Kong

ISBN 0 670 84616 3

Front cover: *Pachystegia insignis,* Marlborough rock
daisy; *Sophora tetraptera,* kowhai; *Hebe speciosa;*
Dracophyllum latifolium.
Back cover: *Pittosporum crassifolium,* karo; *Ranunculus
lyalli,* great mountain buttercup.

CONTENTS

INTRODUCTION

Native plants have fascinated me since an early age. Over the years my horticultural interests have been wide ranging, but that strong interest in the native flora and in particular how it can be used in gardens has always remained with me.

During my late teens I enjoyed the friendship of a talented potter who was a native plants devotee. The garden around his home reflected his love of nature, and displayed a feel for natural design that had been sharpened by expeditions into remote bush, mountain and coastal areas to observe the native flora in a pristine setting.

From him I learnt that our plants are far from dull, a contradiction of an old myth that unfortunately lingers with some gardeners. As well as growing those natives noted for their colourful foliage and flowers, the potter, with his eye for form and texture, was also well aware of the beauty of plants with interesting foliage.

The cool, shady areas of his garden were massed with ferns planted in large groups of one kind, as he had observed them in the wild, creating an expanse of soft-looking green foliage that was delightfully natural and provided a serene spot to escape the heat of summer. Prostrate native plants with small grey, bronze or green foliage linked his designs, spreading out beneath the shrubs and trees and spilling over rocks and onto pathways in a charmingly natural style. Bold-foliaged plants, such as flaxes and the Chatham Island forget-me-not, were made to look more impressive by being placed next to fine-leaved tussock grasses, whose slender foliage sparkled in the sun and swayed with the breeze.

Although his garden was not large, he had allowed room for several strategically placed specimen trees, which provided strong focal points and disguised the odd unwanted view. One was a kauri, which displayed the magnificent pyramidal form and bronze foliage typical of young trees. Also memorable was a rimu, still a comparative youngster at 20 years, its slender, cord-like, light green foliage cascading to the ground. A kowhai completed the trio, its golden blooms announcing the arrival of spring every year.

One of the most rewarding things about a garden of native plants is the regular visits by native birds. My friend never tired of watching the tuis flock to the kowhai as soon as the flowers began to colour, tearing the blooms in their haste to reach the precious nectar within, and becoming increasingly raucous and daring in their aerobatics as they drank their fill.

My friend's enthusiasm for native plants seemed unusual then. Now, some 20 years later, native plants are highly regarded and are grown by many gardeners. Nowhere is this change of attitude more obvious than in the garden centres, which now stock an ever-increasing range of New Zealand natives. In addition there are several specialist native plant nurseries that stock the more unusual, hard-to-get lines as well as those much in demand. These specialist nurseries usually offer a mail-order service that is much appreciated by native plant enthusiasts.

Why have native plants become so popular? There are a number of reasons, the most obvious being that many are indisputably beautiful. Take the kowhai for instance, rated by many overseas authorities as one of the finest flowering trees to be found anywhere. Another drawcard for gardeners, and landscape architects, is the distinctive form possessed by a great number of native plants. Modern architecture is often complemented by the unmistakable outline of a cabbage tree, the bold form of flaxes, the tropical look provided by the huge leaves of the puka, *Meryta sinclairii*, or the strange, inimitable appearance of the lancewoods, *Pseudopanax*.

Dedicated horticulturists who, over the years, have sought out improved forms, and plant breeders who have developed new varieties have also played an important role in popularising native plants. Many of the new varieties, such as the hybrid flaxes, are keenly sought after by gardeners in other parts of

A garden of native plants

the world as well as in New Zealand.

No doubt the interest in native plants will continue to grow, and I hope this book will provide a guide for those gardeners wishing to know more about how to grow native plants in their gardens. I must point out that it is not intended to be a book for the expert, who is already served by several excellent works. Rather, it is a book for the gardener whose love affair with native plants is in its early stages.

NATIVE PLANTS FOR SPECIAL SITUATIONS

NATIVE PLANTS FOR GROUND COVER

Ground-cover plants can transform a garden. They can be used to disguise disagreeable features or to enhance pleasant ones, to reduce loss of moisture from the soil surface, as an aid to maintenance and to stabilise loose soils.

Among native plants there are a number that make interesting and useful ground covers. The majority are notable for their foliage rather than for spectacular flowers or berries, although there are some exceptions such as *Hebe* 'Hartii', which has masses of pale blue flowers, *Acaena microphylla*, noted for its bright red burrs, and *Coprosma acerosa*, with its translucent blue berries.

There are native ground-cover plants for virtually every situation, from the drifting sands of a new beach section to a shaded site beneath trees in an inland garden. Some will spread over a considerable distance or cascade two metres or more down a wall, while others with a more restrained nature can be used as a close-knit cover for small bulbs in a rock garden.

By making full use of native ground covers, one can make the plants in a garden do much of the work. Weed-suppressing cover plants provide a natural means of reducing maintenance by smothering weeds before they have a chance to establish themselves. In some situations an expanse of ground cover can take the place of a grass lawn, thereby doing away with one of the most time-absorbing jobs in a garden.

Ground-cover plants are also useful for keeping the surface of the soil cool during hot weather. This can be of great benefit in sandy soils that heat up quickly in summer. A cover of foliage on sand will significantly reduce the evaporation of soil moisture, creating more favourable conditions for plant growth.

Ground covers also have an important contribution to make to the design of a garden. They enhance the appearance of other plants, particularly if used as a means of emphasising the bolder form and foliage of shrubs and trees. Among many possibilities, a group of flaxes with striped red and cream foliage underplanted with *Coprosma* 'Kirkii' is a striking example of how ground covers and bold shrubs can be combined to good effect.

Grey foliage combines well with a wide range of flower and foliage tones. The small, grey leaves of *Pimelea prostrata* are a good foil to bright colours such as the brilliant red flowers of *Metrosideros carminea*, which in its shrub form has a compact habit. But the colour contrast does not need to be extreme to work well. For example, the subtle combination of the blue-grey leaves of *Hebe albicans* and the small, grey leaves of *Pimelea prostrata* is most effective. Textural contrast can provide as much interest as colour contrast.

The possibilities for creating interesting plant combinations with native ground covers are enormous, and experimenting with combinations of form, colour and texture can be a source of great satisfaction.

Native ground-cover plants are also most effective in combination with brick, stonework or paving. If permitted to sprawl over the edge of a path or onto a paved patio in seemingly carefree fashion, ground covers can create a pleasant air of informality. An interesting idea is to leave the occasional gap in paving for ground covers, but take care that plants grown in such a situation do not become a nuisance by obstructing easy walking or, in the case of sitting-out areas, snagging chairs as they are moved about.

Trailing ground covers spilling over walls or creeping over the edges of steps are always appealing. When paths or driveways are unnaturally straight, prostrate plants are invaluable for a softening effect, and unattractive materials such as concrete can be disguised by ground covers. More pleasing materials such as brick or stone are often enhanced if draped with interesting foliage. Stepping stones, too, gain in appeal when set among a low cover of foliage such as that provided by *Acaena microphylla, Mazus radicans, Pimelea prostrata, Pratia angulata, Scleranthus biflorus*, or *Gunnera prorepens*.

Large ornamental rocks can be interesting garden features. Making them appear as if they belong in the landscape, rather than looking as if they have been brought from afar and dumped in a convenient spot, is the key to their successful use in gardens.

Coprosma 'Prostrata'

NATIVE PLANTS FOR CONTAINERS

Outdoor container plants are popular for adding interest to courtyards, patios and entrance-ways. A number of native plants are well suited to growing in containers as they have the bold, distinctive look that makes for impact. Some natives suitable for container growing have another point in their favour: they will stand more neglect than many of the exotic plants that are popular for this style of gardening.

Few outdoor container plants are as striking as the variegated cabbage tree, *Cordyline australis* 'Albertii', which looks decidedly tropical yet is surprisingly hardy. It looks good all year round and can remain for a long time in a half wine barrel or similar container, requiring nothing more than an occasional feeding and a thorough watering every now and again when it does not rain regularly. One problem that occurs at times with this and other cabbage trees is insect damage to the foliage, but this can be controlled if an insecticide is used at the first sign of trouble.

Other natives that provide a bold, tropical look in containers include *Meryta sinclairii*, puka, with its huge, shiny, green, paddle-shaped leaves, and the flaxes, which are great in big containers, especially those with colourful foliage and upright leaves. *Pseudopanax* are also spectacular, particularly the *lessonii* hybrids and 'Gold Splash', with its green and gold leaves.

Native plants do not have to be large to look striking in containers. The tussock grass *Carex lucida*, noted for its long and thick, thread-like, coppery bronze foliage, is a delight in a tall container, which allows its cascading habit to be shown off to advantage. *Astelia chathamica* is another unusual container subject. It has the spiky form characteristic of the flaxes

Thoughtful positioning is required, and ground covers planted so they swathe the base of a large rock can do much to make it blend with the surroundings. Prostrate native plants with distinctive foliage, such as *Rubus parvus*, can be most interesting when used for this purpose. Ground-cover manukas and coprosmas also have great possibilities for combining with rocks.

For plants to be successful as ground covers, it is not essential that they have a prostrate habit of growth. Large-leaved perennial native plants such as *Arthropodium cirratum*, renga renga, and *Myosotidium hortensia*, the Chatham Island forget-me-not, can be most effective as ground covers when planted in large groups.

Many of the native grasses available from nurseries also make good ground covers. They can be used as fillers among shrubs, on the edge of a border or as a mass planting of a single species, or a group of different grasses can be intermingled in charming fashion. The fine-foliaged kinds, such as *Carex lucida*, have a gracefulness that makes them well suited to numerous situations.

but the foliage is silver and the plant is tidier. The old foliage tends to shrivel up and is not conspicuous, unlike the flaxes, which need a trimming operation at regular intervals to keep them looking respectable.

The choice of container plants for seaside gardens is often rather limited because of salt winds and dry conditions. The variegated Kermadec pohutukawa, *Metrosideros kermadecensis* 'Variegata', stands up well to harsh coastal conditions, looks superb and can remain in a large container such as a half wine barrel for years.

In small gardens containers provide the opportunity to grow some of the tall native trees that would soon become a problem if planted out in the ground. Karakas, for instance, make grand container plants. The magnificent kauri can also be grown in a large container for a few years. It looks striking and can be quite a talking point when featured on a patio or at an entrance-way.

The soil used in containers should be reasonably light and porous. Soil straight from the garden may be too heavy, although it can be made more suitable by mixing it with river sand and organic material such as peat, compost or leaf mould. One of the most satisfactory growing media is a mixture of 60 per cent peat and 40 per cent coarse river sand. The ready-mixed potting mixes available from garden centres have the advantage of being convenient and well tested, although they may seem expensive by comparison with a home-made soil mixture.

Good drainage is important for container plants. Ensure that there are efficient drainage holes in the bottom of the container. A layer of gravel on the bottom of the container is often used to assist with drainage, although this should not be necessary if using a porous potting mixture such as sand and peat.

Regular watering is also important for container plants, because their confined roots cannot call on water deep in the soil as plants in the garden can. They also require regular feeding, but this need not be a chore if one of the long-lasting, slow-release fertilisers is used.

Flaxes (*Phormium*) make handsome container plants.

NATIVE PLANTS FOR CONTAINERS

Agathis australis, Astelia chathamica (some other *Astelia* species too), *Brachyglottis repanda, Brachyglottis repanda* 'Purpurea', *Carex lucida* (some other *Carex* species too), *Cordyline australis, Cordyline australis* 'Albertii', *Cordyline australis* 'Purpurea', *Corynocarpus laevigatus* (variegated cultivars are especially suitable), *Entelea arborescens, Fuchsia procumbens, Griselinia littoralis* 'Taranaki Cream', *Griselinia littoralis* 'Variegata', *Griselinia lucida, Libertia peregrinans, Meryta sinclairii, Metrosideros carminea* (shrub form), *Metrosideros kermadecensis* 'Variegata', *Phormium* (species and hybrids), *Pisonia brunonianum* 'Variegata', *Pseudopanax* (all species), *Xeronema callistemon.*

NATIVE PLANTS TO GROW IN SHADE

Most gardens have an area of shade, but sometimes these areas are difficult to garden because the soil is dry, or they are cold and draughty because the wind funnels between bare trunks of tall trees. Shaded areas can also be sheltered and have rich, moist soils. Whatever the case may be, there are native plants that are well suited to the conditions and can make a shaded garden a place of beauty.

Shaded gardens with good moist soils are ideal for native ferns. An area planted in ferns can be a delightfully tranquil portion of garden, a lovely contrast to brighter colours in other parts of the garden and a place to escape from summer heat and glare. There is a great range of native ferns, from tiny creeping plants to the majestic tree ferns.

Unfortunately not all gardens in shade are suitable for ferns. Where the soil is dry and there is dense shade, as is often the case beneath tall trees, the range of plants that will grow successfully tends to be limited. However, there are some tough natives that will perform well under such conditions. One of the most reliable is the versatile karo, *Pittosporum crassifolium*, which is better known as an exceptionally hardy coastal tree. Karo is useful as a ground-draught break beneath tall trees that have bare trunks for some distance above ground level. It can be maintained as a hedge or allowed to develop to its natural form.

Also suitable for dry shade are *Brachyglottis repanda* and *Pseudopanax laetum*, both of which are handsome foliage shrubs. Kawa kawa, *Macropiper excelsum*, is another candidate for dry shade. It is often dismissed as being little better than a weed because it grows with such ease and self-sows freely, but where conditions are tough such characteristics are to be welcomed. Kawa kawa remains bushy in shade and is excellent for providing shelter and privacy.

One of the most colourful natives for shade is *Pisonia brunonianum* 'Variegatum'. Its large leaves have beautiful cream and grey-green variegations and the new growths are tinged with pink. Unfortunately, the variegated pisonia is rather tender and is only suitable for growing outdoors in milder districts. It requires a reasonably rich, well-drained soil.

Another native with dramatic foliage that will grow in shade is puka, *Meryta sinclairii*. It is usually seen in the open, although its success is limited by its very tenderness to frost. When positioned beneath the shelter of overhead trees, however, it can be grown in gardens that experience moderate frosts. Puka makes a delightful contrast with bushy variegated coprosmas such as *C. repens* 'Silver Queen', which also does well in light shade.

There are several native plants with showy flowers that will grow well in light shade. One of the most appealing is the small shrub *Rhabdothamnus solandri*, which has pretty red flowers over many months. *Arthropodium cirratum*, which will grow in various situations including light shade, has pretty white flowers on long stems and makes a great show in mid-summer. Although it is frost tender, it can be grown in cold areas if protected by a canopy of overhead foliage.

When planting in dry shade, it will pay to dig in a general fertiliser plus some organic matter such as compost. After planting, water thoroughly and, if possible, water again periodically during the first season. This will make it easier for the plants to become established. Bear in mind that small plants usually adapt more easily to difficult conditions than large specimens.

NATIVE PLANTS TO GROW IN SHADE

Ackama rosaefolia, Alseuosmia microphylla, Arthropodium cirratum, Brachyglottis repanda, Coprosma australis, Coprosma repens, Coprosma repens 'Silver Queen', *Coprosma* 'Williamsii Variegata', *Cordyline australis, Cordyline banksii, Cordyline indivisa, Cordyline kaspar, Corokia buddleioides, Dacrydium cupressinum, Dianella nigra, Earina autumnalis, Earina mucronata,* ferns, *Fuchsia excorticata, Griselinia lucida, Hedycarya arborea, Jovellana sinclairii, Libertia grandiflora, Lophomyrtus bullata, Lophomyrtus* 'Gloriosa' *Macropiper excelsum, Macropiper excelsum* var. *majus, Meryta sinclairii, Myosotidium hortensia, Paratrophis microphylla* 'Charles Devonshire', *Pisonia brunoniana* 'Variegata', *Pittosporum crassifolium, Pittosporum eugenioides, Pittosporum ralphii, Pittosporum ralphii* 'Variegatum' *Pittosporum tenuifolium, Pseudopanax* 'Adiantifolium', *Pseudopanax crassifolium, Pseudopanax laetum, Pseudopanax lessonii, Pseudowintera colorata, Rhabdothamnus solandri, Rhopalostylis sapida.*

Myosotidium hortensia

NATIVE PLANTS FOR BEACH GARDENS

Plants for coastal gardens can be loosely grouped into two categories: those that will tolerate very exposed situations — the shelter plants — and those that will grow happily in beach gardens where there is some protection from the full force of gales blowing in from the sea. In both categories there are many handsome native plants. Some, such as the pohutukawa, are deservedly famous for their resistance to salt winds and their ability to grow in the most inhospitable of places. But there are many others that can make a coastal garden more pleasant by providing shelter from the elements. One of the most notable of these is karo, *Pittosporum crassifolium*, which is as tough as the pohutukawa in most situations and often performs better than it when planted as the first line of defence against sea gales.

The marvellous thing about the pohutukawa is that it has such beautiful flowers, which occur at the height of the summer holiday season. Pohutukawas can take all sorts of abuse. Mature trees can be cut to near ground level and they will soon shoot into new growth again. They can also be kept as trimmed hedges if desired, but this tree has such an attractive form that it seems a pity not to allow it to develop naturally wherever possible.

Metrosideros excelsa is the most suitable pohutukawa for planting where the conditions are exposed. *M. kermadecensis*, the Kermadec pohutukawa, is not as tough and is not suitable for very exposed situations. With a little shelter, it makes a handsome tree for beach gardens, and its habit of flowering at odd times throughout the year means that it provides colour when *M. excelsa* is not in flower. The variegated Kermadec pohutukawa, *M. kermadecensis* 'Variegata', is a handsome foliage tree for beach gardens. It is just as wind hardy as the green-leaved form and makes an attractive and tough container plant for gardens near the sea.

One complaint that is often voiced concerning native plants in coastal gardens is that they are slow growing. Certainly there are exotic plants that will grow faster in beach gardens than natives, but it should be remembered that some of the most rapid growers tend to have a short life span, whereas the natives, which take a little longer to become established, are often noted for their longevity. There are some native plants suited to the coast that grow comparatively quickly. *Olearia traversii*, for instance, will make rapid growth, even in pure sand.

There are means of speeding up the rate of growth of plants in beach gardens. Watering during dry weather for the first few seasons will help plants to establish themselves more readily. When watering, it is no good just damping down the surface; a thorough soaking is necessary if it is to have much effect. Organic matter mixed with the sand will help it to absorb water more readily, and a mulch of organic material such as seaweed or a layer of stones around the plants will help to keep the sand cool and slow down the loss of moisture. A general fertiliser, added to the sand at planting time and again the following spring, will also help to boost growth, but do not feed the plants excessively or too much soft growth may result. Keeping weeds down around young plants will also help them to get off to a good start as weeds can smother young plants and they are also greedy competitors for moisture and nutrients.

It is better to start with small plants when trying to establish shelter in coastal gardens. Large specimens are often pot bound and have a much harder time adapting to the conditions than small plants, which will usually grow much faster. Artificial shelter such as scrim or one of the new wind-break cloths stretched between stakes, or brush or any number of readily available natural materials will also be beneficial.

Once shelter is established in a beach garden, it is astonishing what a great range of plants can be grown. The following list contains plants that are particularly well suited to growing near the coast and will succeed with a minimum of attention. There are other native plants that will do well in beach gardens, but success will depend on how exposed the site is and how much attention they can be given.

Pohutukawa, *Metrosideros excelsa*, an outstanding tree for growing in exposed coastal sites

NATIVE CLIMBING PLANTS

The number of climbing native plants suitable for gardens is small but among them are some colourful and distinctive plants. *Clematis paniculata* is a gem of the native flora and is well known and highly regarded, both in New Zealand and overseas. Its pure white flowers have a daintiness that the large-flowered hybrid clematis cannot match, and it looks striking when it is allowed to twine through a tree, as it does in nature.

A much more vigorous climber useful for covering a wall or growing over a pergola or archway is *Tecomanthe speciosa*, a comparative newcomer to cultivation. It has striking foliage and provides a special character for gardens. The flowers, which occur in early winter, are large and most unusual, and attract native birds such as the tui.

The most colourful native climber is undoubtedly *Metrosideros carminea*, akakura, which has carmine red flowers sought after by the nectar-eating native birds. The blooms are produced in spring and are so thick that the foliage is often hidden, making a dazzling display. *M. carminea* climbs by means of small aerial roots, in the same manner as ivy, and it will climb anything that affords a reasonable grip, making it useful for covering unsightly things in the garden such as old tanks, lamp posts, stumps or walls.

The native passionfruit is little known in cultivation yet its orange fruits make a great show. *Parsonsia* is another native climber that is paid little attention by gardeners, perhaps because its flowers are not spectacularly colourful. However, they have a delicious scent, are most attractive and occur in thick clusters that make the vines sag under the weight.

Many of the native climbers are charming plants with a character all their own. It is surprising that they are not planted more, for they have much to offer the discerning gardener.

Clematis paniculata

NATIVE PLANTS WITH DRAMATIC FORM

Gardeners are often attracted by the distinctive appearance of many native plants, which makes them an ideal choice for planting where a dramatic effect is desired, such as against a house, on a patio, in containers, around a swimming pool or in association with modern architecture.

Some natives that look decidedly tropical are actually very hardy to cold. The flaxes, most of the *Cordyline* species and some of the *Pseudopanax* come into this category, and can look splendid when used in imaginative landscaping projects, even in colder parts of the country. In mild areas the huge, dark green leaves of puka, *Meryta sinclairii*, make this tree popular for planting in various situations. It looks marvellous standing out boldly as an individual specimen in a lawn or combined with other native plants with striking foliage such as *Pisonia brunoniana* 'Variegata', or variegated-foliage coprosmas such as *Coprosma repens* 'Silver Queen'.

Flaxes provide a dramatic effect, and among the numerous modern hybrids are some of the most striking foliage plants to be found anywhere. *Astelia chathamica* is a dramatic and unusual plant that looks like a silver-leaved flax. At present it is still something of a connoisseur's plant, but it is being used more frequently in landscaping. ·

Native plants do not have to be big to make an impact. The erect leaves of *Libertia peregrinans* are no more than 30 centimetres high, yet their form is so distinctive that they stand out from afar. Plants such as this are ideal for growing in combination with rounded stones or through a low, small-leaved ground-cover plant such as one of the purple-leaved acaenas or the grey-foliaged *Pimelea prostrata*. Native tussock grasses, with their fine foliage, are ideal for combining with bold-leaved natives.

The tree ferns are often overlooked when plants with dramatic form are being sought, which is a pity, for they are beautiful and have a bold, tropical appearance that is hard to equal. Some species stand up surprisingly well to wind and adapt to a wide range of conditions. Where the climate is reasonably mild and the location is sheltered from frost, the king fern,

The bold form of flax (*Phormium*) is emphasised by a small-leaved ground cover such as *Coprosma* 'Kirkii'.

Marattia salicina, is an exciting plant to grow. Its luxuriant, shiny green fronds look superb against a light-stained wood wall or combined with other distinctive foliage plants such as *Pisonia brunonianum* 'Variegatum', *Rhopalostylis sapida* (nikau), tree ferns or non-natives such as medium-sized bamboos.

One distinctive but neglected plant that deserves attention is the weeping broom, *Chordospartium stevensonii*. It is a small, leafless tree that is easy to grow, but it looks insignificant during its early years and one must be patient and allow it time to develop its full potential.

Any list of native plants with distinctive form and foliage would not be complete without the unique *Pseudopanax*. Species such as *Pseudopanax crassifolius*, the lancewood, and the lesser-known but even more dramatic *Pseudopanax ferox*, the toothed lancewood, are exciting trees for use in landscaping, as are *Pseudopanax laetum* and the hybrid *Pseudopanax* 'Adiantifolium'.

NATIVE PLANTS WITH DRAMATIC FORM

Arthropodium cirratum. Astelia chathamica (and other astelias). *Brachyglottis rangiora, Brachyglottis rangiora* 'Purpurea', *Carex lucida* (and other *Carex* species), *Carmichaelia* 'Williamsii', *Chordospartium stevensonii, Cordyline australis, Cordyline australis* 'Albertii', *Cordyline australis* 'Purpurea', *Cordyline banksii, Cordyline indivisa, Cordyline kaspar, Dracophyllum* (all species), *Entelea arborescens*, ferns (in particular *Marattia salicina* and tree ferns), *Griselinia lucida, Hoheria populnea* 'Alba Variegata', *Libertia peregrinans, Macropiper excelsum* var. *majus, Meryta sinclairii, Myosotidium hortensia, Phormium* species and hybrids, *Pseudopanax* 'Adiantifolium', *Pseudopanax crassifolius, Pseudopanax ferox, Pseudopanax* 'Gold Splash', *Pseudopanax laetum, Pseudopanax lessonii* hybrids, *Pisonia brunoniana* 'Variegata', *Rhopalostylis sapida, Tecomanthe speciosa, Vitex lucens.*

NATIVE PLANTS FOR DAMP SOILS

In some gardens there are areas that are constantly damp or wet. Such conditions do not suit many plants, but there are some attractive natives that will grow well in soils that are always damp, and a few, such as *Dacrycarpus dacrydioides* and *Phormium tenax*, will actually grow in shallow water.

In large country gardens there is sometimes a swampy area of ground inhabited by clumps of flax. Every effort should be made to retain such areas in their natural state for they have a special beauty that cannot easily be duplicated. Swampland inhabited by kahikatea should also be retained wherever possible and treasured for its special character.

When planting trees that will tolerate 'wet feet' in an area that is under water, it will be necessary to either make a raised area for them to grow in or divert the water until they are established. They cannot be simply planted in a hole in a waterlogged spot and be expected to flourish.

Flaxes with a weeping habit of growth, such as *Phormium cookianum* 'Tricolor', are charming when planted right at the water's edge. A memorable scene is created when the tips of the leaves brush the water and it becomes hard to tell where the foliage stops and the watery reflection starts.

Hebe X *franciscana* 'Blue Gem' grows well in dry soils.

NATIVE PLANTS FOR DAMP SOILS

Cordyline australis, Cordyline banksii, Cordyline indivisa, Dacrydium bidwillii, Dacrydium biforme, Dacrydium cupressinum, Dicksonia fibrosa, Dicksonia squarrosa, Elaeocarpus dentatus, Fuchsia excorticata, Hoheria glabrata, Laurelia novae-zelandiae, Phormium spp., *Plagianthus betulinus, Plagianthus divaricatus, Podocarpus dacrydioides, Rhopalostylis sapida, Senecio huntii, Weinmannia racemosa.*

NATIVE PLANTS FOR DRY SOILS

Many gardens have an area of dry soil. In some cases it is a limited space, such as beneath overhanging eaves, or the whole garden may be on a dry, sun-baked site with poor soil. Whatever the case, there are some most attractive native plants that will grow surprisingly well in such conditions.

Although the plants in the following list will tolerate dry soils, they still need attention at planting time. It will pay to add a general fertiliser and organic matter such as peat or compost, and water the plants thoroughly after they are put into the ground and during the first season. Once the plants are making good growth they can be left to fend for themselves, but if they are ignored from the start, progress is likely to be disappointingly slow.

Pachystegias are rugged and are worth growing for their foliage almost as much as for the delightful daisy flowers that cover the bushes in summer. The variegated-foliage cultivars of *Coprosma repens* are exciting plants that provide a bold splash of colour. The sprawling habit of *Coprosma repens* 'Variegata' makes it a striking subject to use as a contrast to trees with a pronounced upright habit, such as *Cordyline australis.*

Some of the hebes thrive in dry soils. *Hebe* X *franciscana* 'Blue Gem' and *Hebe speciosa* are both beautiful, free flowering shrubs that relish hot, dry situations. Less well known as a plant for dry soils is *Hebe hulkeana*. It is often grown in rich, moist soils with rather disappointing results, but when planted in a light, dryish soil in an open, sunny situation, it produces a stunning display of long-stemmed flowers.

One of the most spectacular shrubs for growing in dry soils is kumarahou, *Pomaderris kumeraho*. In spring it is covered with golden yellow flowers. Unfortunately kumarahou is short lived but it grows rapidly and flowers freely from an early age. Kaka beak, *Clianthus puniceus*, is another colourful and free-flowering shrub for dry soils.

When it comes to trees that will grow well in dry soils, the pohutukawa, *Metrosideros excelsa*, must rate as one of the finest. The only thing that limits where it will grow is frost. The variegated Kermadec pohutukawa, *Metrosideros kermadecensis* 'Variegata', is one of the finest variegated shrubs for growing in dry soils.

NATIVE PLANTS FOR DRY SOILS

Acaena microphylla, Aciphylla (all species), *Brachyglottis repanda, Brachyglottis repanda* 'Purpurea', *Cassinia* (all species), *Clianthus puniceus* and cultivars, *Coprosma acerosa. Coprosma australis, Coprosma brunnea* X 'Kirkii', *Coprosma* 'Kirkii', *Coprosma* 'Kirkii Variegata', *Coprosma* 'Kiwi Gold', *Coprosma* 'Prostrata', *Coprosma repens* and cultivars,

---

NATIVE PLANTS FOR THE FLOWER ARRANGER

The native flora provides few flowers that are good for floral work, but there is a richness of foliage that more than makes up for this. Plants such as the variegated *Lophomyrtus* species and the hybrid flaxes, with colourful striped leaves, are a marvellous source of foliage material throughout the year. Many hectares around the country are devoted to growing these plants to supply local and export markets, but for most of us, several different plants are sufficient to provide foliage whenever required.

The foliage of *Pittosporum tenuifolium* cultivars has long been popular for picking, and the new and highly attractive cultivars offer even more possibilities to the floral artist. A mixed hedge of some of these pretty variegated-foliage pittosporums provides a wealth of floral material.

Less well-known foliage plants that can provide interesting material for flower arrangements include the astelias, particularly *Astelia* 'Silver Spear', with its silvery green, flax-like leaves, the young foliage of the red beech, *Nothofagus fusca*, and the colourful winter foliage of the kamahi, *Weinmannia racemosa*.

The brightly coloured foliage of *Pseudopanax* 'Gold Splash' and the stiff leaves of *Libertia peregrinans* also offer many possibilities for the imaginative floral arranger.

The flowers of the hybrid manukas are outstanding for floral arrangements. Some last better in water than others and you may have to experiment a little to discover which are the most suitable. The various cultivars flower at different times from mid-winter to late spring. Curious flowers such as those of the rewarewa, *Knightia excelsa*, are useful in bold flower arrangements.

A number of native plants also provide interesting material for dried flower arrangements. The flower-heads of the native grasses are useful for this, as are the seed-pods of the flaxes and some species of *Libertia*. The dainty seed-heads of the tussocks, such as *Carex flagellifera*, are surprisingly beautiful when dried, and the everlasting flowers of *Gnaphalium keriense* and the larger-flowered forms of *Helichrysum bellidioides* have potential for small dried arrangements.

The ornamental berries of *Pseudopanax, Lophomyrtus, Corokia* and others have their uses too and often they are available during autumn and winter when floral material is in short supply. The brilliant red seed-capsules of *Dodonaea viscosa* 'Purpurea' are also striking in flower arrangements.

NATIVE PLANTS TO ATTRACT BIRDS

One of the pleasures of growing native plants is that many of them attract native birds to our gardens. The most famous bird attracters are the kowhais, *Sophora microphylla* and *Sophora tetraptera*. The nectar-seeking birds such as tuis, bellbirds and waxeyes delight in the golden blooms of the kowhais, and the tuis in particular provide marvellous entertain-

The native wood pigeon is attracted to the berries of nikau, *Rhopalostylis sapida*.

ment as they flit from flower to flower and fill the garden with their melodious song.

Puriri, *Vitex lucens*, is a marvellous tree for native birds. It is seldom without fruit or flowers and is a favourite tree of the wood pigeon. Other tall, berry-producing native trees that attract wood pigeons include the pigeonwood, *Hedycarya arborea*, karaka, *Corynocarpus laevigatus*, kahikatea, *Podocarpus dacrydioides*, miro *Podocarpus ferrugineus* and nikau, *Rhopalostylis sapida*.

Tecomanthe speciosa, one of the most ornamental native climbing plants, also attracts native birds. Its large pale yellow flowers occur in early winter, a time when food is scarce for birds. The climbing ratas (*Metrosideros*) also attract the nectar eaters, and *M. carminea* in particular is a spectacular garden plant.

In small gardens there are a number of shrubs that can be planted to attract native birds. *Clianthus puniceus*, or kaka beak as it is well known, flowers over a long period, and waxeyes and other birds have a great liking for the colourful flowers. The flowers of flax, *Phormium*, also attract the nectar feeders, as do those of the dwarf kowhai, *Sophora tetraptera* 'Gnome', an excellent plant for growing where there is limited space.

NATIVE PLANTS TO ATTRACT BIRDS

Alectryon excelsus, Beilschmiedia tawa, Clianthus puniceus, Coprosma australis, Corynocarpus laevigatus, Fuchsia excorticata, Hedycarya arborea, Knightia excelsa, Lophomyrtus spp., *Melicytis ramiflorus, Metrosideros* (all species), *Phormium* (both species plus hybrids), *Podocarpus dacrydioides, Podocarpus ferrugineus, Pseudopanax* (all species), *Rhopalostylis sapida, Sophora* (all species), *Tecomanthe speciosa, Vitex lucens.*

NATIVE SPECIMEN TREES

Specimen trees are those that possess sufficient character or beauty to stand alone in a garden and to serve as a focal point. Specimen trees are planted in situations such as lawns and farm paddocks, among low-growing shrubs or ground covers, in courtyards or beside houses.

When deciding what to plant as a specimen tree, there are several points to consider. One of the most obvious is suitability for the soil and climate; another is the ultimate size. The rate of growth should also be taken into account; it can be frustrating to watch a tree grow at a rate of inches per year when a large tree is required for a feeling of maturity or to provide scale.

Take care where you plant a tree. A wide-spreading tree can become a problem if positioned too close to a building or neighbouring property. Take the angle of the sun at different times of the year into account, too, and make sure that a tall-growing tree is not going to block out sunlight from your own or neighbouring properties.

A number of native trees make outstanding specimen trees. Where there is room, the mighty kauri, *Agathis australis*, is superb. In smaller gardens

Podocarpus totara 'Aurea'

there is often room for smaller trees such as *Pseudopanax crassifolius* or *Pseudopanax ferox*.

Adventurous gardeners gain a great deal of pleasure from using some of the lesser-known yet very distinctive native trees as specimens in their gardens. *Hoheria sexstylosa*, the long-leaved lacebark, is seldom encountered in gardens yet it is of more interest than many widely planted exotics. *Chordospartium stevensonii* is another native tree that remains neglected by gardeners. Admittedly it takes some years before it fully develops its fascinating character, but the wait is well worth it, for this leafless tree is unique.

NATIVE SPECIMEN TREES

Agathis australis, Alectryon excelsus, Aristotelia serrata, Chordospartium stevensonii, Cordyline australis and cultivars, *Cordyline kaspar, Corynocarpus laevigatus* 'Variegatus', *Cyathea medullaris, Dacrydium cupressinum, Hoheria angustifolia, Hoheria sexstylosa, Knightia excelsa, Leptospermum ericoides, Meryta sinclairii, Metrosideros excelsa, Metrosideros kermadecensis* and variegated cultivars, *Myoporum laetum, Nothofagus* (all), *Olearia albida* var. *angulata, Pittosporum eugenioides* 'Variegatum', *Podocarpus dacrydioides, Podocarpus ferrugineus, Podocarpus hallii, Podocarpus totara, Podocarpus totara* 'Aurea', *Pseudopanax* 'Adiantifolium', *Pseudopanax crassifolius, Pseudopanax ferox, Rhopalostylis sapida, Sophora microphylla, Sophora tetraptera, Vitex lucens.*

NATIVE PLANTS FOR HEDGES

Hedges can perform a number of different functions. Their role as providers of privacy and shelter is well known, but hedges can also provide a fascinating architectural effect, and openings in hedges provide a marvellous opportunity for framing views. Bear in mind that hedges do not have to be planted in straight rows when they are used within the garden. A closely trimmed, curving hedge can be as fascinating as a skilfully designed wall.

Hedges do have their disadvantages, not least of which is the necessity for frequent trimming to keep them in shape. If a garden is intended to be easily maintained, then it will pay to look at alternatives to hedges such as a mixed planting of shrubs or trees. A combination of shrubs and trees can have several advantages over a hedge, including a more natural appearance and a greater ability to provide shelter as well as requiring very little attention.

Among the many native plants suitable for hedging, there are plants for virtually every situation. From windswept beach gardens to sheltered inland properties, from dry sands to waterlogged soils, in sun or shade, there are native plants that will perform well and look attractive as hedges.

The golden totara, *Podocarpus totara* 'Aurea', makes a hedge that is more ornamental than most exotics. *Corokia cotoneaster* can be trimmed to form a remarkably narrow hedge that is most attractive and marvellous for small gardens. For hedges with a bright splash of colour, the variegated coprosmas, especially *Coprosma* 'Silver Queen', are superb. They can be trained into all sorts of shapes and grow with ease in poor, dry soils. The purple akeake, *Dodonaea viscosa* 'Purpurea', makes a striking hedge with its purple-red leaves, a foliage colour quite distinct from other hedging plants.

The adventurous gardener can have fun choosing less-common native plants for hedges. *Lophomyrtus* hybrids with beautiful foliage colours, for example *Lophomyrtus* 'Kathryn' and *Lophomyrtus* 'Gloriosa', the newer *Pittosporum tenuifolium* cultivars with gold and silver variegated leaves, the beeches (*Nothofagus*), kamahi (*Weinmannia racemosa*) and others make hedges that are both delightful and unusual.

When planting a hedge it pays to prepare the site beforehand. Cultivate the site thoroughly and incorporate a general fertiliser. Most soils will also benefit from the addition of organic matter such as compost or peat. The plants should be set reasonably close together so they will form a close barrier; in most instances a spacing of 75 to 90 centimetres will be satisfactory.

Make sure that hedging plants do not dry out while they are waiting to be put into the ground, and water them well immediately after planting unless heavy rain is imminent. Remember that a hedge that is kept clear of weeds during its first few years will establish far quicker than one that has to compete with weeds for moisture and nutrients.

Trimming of a hedge should usually start in the second year after planting. Any leggy plants should have their centres cut out at planting time.

Corokia cotoneaster is a versatile and tough hedging plant.

NATIVE PLANTS FOR HEDGES

Coprosma repens and its variegated-foliage cultivars, *Corokia cotoneaster*, *Corokia* hybrids, *Corynocarpus laevigatus*, *Dodonaea viscosa*, *Dodonaea viscosa* 'Purpurea', *Griselinia littoralis*, *Griselinia littoralis* 'Variegata', *Lophomyrtus* 'Gloriosa', *Lophomyrtus* 'Kathryn', *Metrosideros excelsa*, *Metrosideros kermadecensis* 'Variegata', *Myoporum laetum*, *Nothofagus fusca*, *Nothofagus menziesii*, *Nothofagus truncata*, *Olearia albida*, *Olearia paniculata*, *Olearia traversii*, *Phormium tenax* (untrimmed hedge), *Pittosporum crassifolium*, *Pittosporum eugenioides*, *Pittosporum ralphii*, *Pittosporum tenuifolium* cultivars, *Plagianthus divaricatus*, *Podocarpus hallii*, *Podocarpus nivalis*, *Podocarpus totara*, *Podocarpus totara* 'Aurea', *Pomaderris apetala*, *Weinmannia racemosa*.

Metrosideros excelsa

NATIVE PLANTS FOR GARDENS

NATIVE PLANTS FOR GARDENS

ACAENA
Rosaceae

Among the native *Acaena* species are some superb mat-forming plants that are particularly useful for rock gardens and as ground covers. They are notable for their colourful, burr-like seed-heads and close-knit, ferny foliage. Acaenas tend to grow quickly and will spread over a wide area, but their wanderlust is easily checked with a sharp spade. A large patch of acaena covered with red seed-heads is a striking sight, and a sunny, well-drained situation will produce the best display of seed-heads. Some *Acaena* species (not those popular in gardens) are a serious weed on rough grazing country and are spread by seed-heads clinging to the wool of sheep and goats by means of the sharp barbs.

Acaenas are easily propagated by separating and lifting rooted runners. They can also be grown from seed, although the former method must be used to be sure of perpetuating selected colour forms and hybrids.

Acaena inermis

Selected forms of this species have beautiful coloured foliage in shades of purple to bronze. It makes a good ground cover.

Acaena microphylla

One of the best-known species in cultivation, *Acaena microphylla* has greenish brown leaves and round, red, spiky seed-heads, which are produced in summer. When plants are growing strongly the seed-heads are often so numerous that the foliage is hidden.

There are other worthwhile species, as well as some attractive hybrids.

ACIPHYLLA
Umbelliferae

There are approximately 40 species of *Aciphylla* native to New Zealand. Most have extremely sharp points to the leaves, a major reason why they are not grown more widely, but they are unusual plants and the

Acaena microphylla

Acaena microphylla makes a spectacular ground cover.

dwarf species in particular make striking subjects for rock gardens.

Male and female flowers are carried on separate plants. All aciphyllas must have excellent drainage, and they usually grow well in rock gardens and raised beds with light soil, but they can also be grown in containers. Full sun is desirable, but aciphyllas are very hardy to cold.

Aciphylla species

Some species are available from mail-order nurseries specialising in native plants; they are not usually sold in garden centres.

Aciphylla aurea
Golden Spaniard

This is one of the larger and more attractive species, with a huge golden yellow flower-head that often reaches a height of one metre. Flowering time is from December to January. The yellowish green foliage has sharp points and the flower stem has very sharp bracts. The golden Spaniard requires careful placement in the garden because of the dangerously spiny foliage, but if it can be accommodated in a large rock garden, it makes a striking feature plant.

Aciphylla monroi
Pigmy speargrass

A small tufted plant, with four to six leaflets making up each leaf. Although the leaves are quite soft, they have sharp tips. The flowers are white and are borne above the foliage on stems up to 30 centimetres high. Flowering time is from December to January. *Aciphylla monroi* is slow growing and makes a most

attractive subject for a rock garden or for a container. One of the most reliable species in cultivation.

Other notable dwarf species are *A. simplex*, which forms a dense cushion of coppery foliage about 15 centimetres high; *A. spedenii*, a slow-growing species with red tipped, blue-green leaves and white flowers; *A. dobsonii*, another slow grower, which forms a cushion of prickly green foliage.

There are a number of other aciphyllas worthy of a place in gardens, and usually it is the smaller species that prove the most satisfactory.

Propagation is by seed.

ACKAMA
Cunoniaceae

One species of *Ackama* is native to New Zealand. Two other species occur in Australia and New Guinea.

Ackama rosaefolia
Makamaka

A handsome small tree with light green, shiny, graceful foliage resembling that of the rose. The undersides of the leaves have an attractive reddish tinge. Makamaka has a spreading habit of growth and at times is more like a large bushy shrub than a tree. In spring bunches of small, cream-coloured flowers are produced in great abundance. As they age, the flowers turn pale red and they remain on the tree for some time in this state.

Makamaka will grow in sun or shade and seems to thrive in most soil types, providing there is good drainage. It is an attractive foliage tree that stands out very well when grown as an isolated specimen. If necessary, it can be trimmed to keep it to a desired height or shape. It is hardy to only light frosts. Where heavy frosts are experienced, it can sometimes be grown by positioning it beneath the protective canopy of tall trees.

In nature it occurs in lowland forests of Northland, often growing alongside towai, *Weinmannia silvicola*, to which it is similar in many respects. The seedlings of both trees are very hard to tell apart.

Makamaka is usually propagated by seed although it can also be raised from semi-hardwood cuttings.

AGATHIS
Araucariaceae

The only species of *Agathis* that occurs in New Zealand is the well-known kauri, *Agathis australis*, which ranks among the most majestic trees of the world.

Agathis australis
Kauri

Although the kauri occurs in nature only in the far north of the North Island, it can be grown in most lowland areas of New Zealand if provided with a sheltered situation. Eventually this tree becomes a forest giant, but many years go by before it reaches a great size. The huge trees that are such a tourist attraction in Northland are many hundreds of years old.

During their early years kauri trees have a most pleasing upright habit of growth and distinctive bronze foliage. The leaves become green as the trees mature. One kauri tree makes a striking specimen in a garden, or if there is room, a group of kauris can be planted as a dramatic feature. In some large gardens the owners have planted a woodland of kauri trees, creating a feature that will be enjoyed by many future generations.

Kauri trees grow readily in an average garden soil. During the first few seasons the young trees will need protection from anything more than a light frost. Trees should be watered during periods of drought. Contrary to popular opinion, they are not a good choice for planting in dry soils.

Propagation is by seed.

Agathis australis, kauri

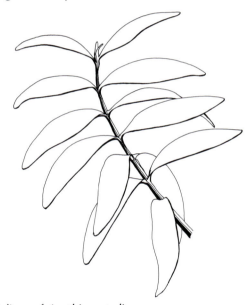

Young foliage of *Agathis australis*.

ALECTRYON
Sapindaceae

There are two New Zealand species of *Alectryon*. *A. excelsus*, titoki, is a well-known tree both in gardens and in the wild. The other species, *A. grandis*, is little known and occurs naturally only on the Three Kings Islands.

Alectryon excelsus
Titoki

A handsome tree with shining pinnate leaves, rounded form and a dark trunk. It is popular as a specimen in gardens and also makes a good street tree. Titoki usually grows to five or six metres in gardens. The tiny flowers are borne on the ends of the branches in panicles up to 30 centimetres long. Often they go unnoticed among the leaves. The small fruits that follow the flowers are most ornamental when they ripen. The hard, brown capsule splits open to reveal a shiny black seed embedded in a brilliant scarlet, fleshy coating. The fruits usually take a year to ripen, therefore flowers and ripe fruits are often seen on the tree together in early summer.

Titoki is only moderately frost hardy. Young trees especially will require frost protection until they are established. An average to rich, well-drained soil is ideal. Shelter from strong winds is also desirable. In very exposed situations there are many other natives that will prove more suitable. In the garden, titoki should be allowed room to develop its natural form; if crowded in among other trees, it tends to be drawn up and become straggly. As a shade tree for a lawn or a bold specimen in a border, it is most attractive. The leaves bear a resemblance to the European ash, and it is sometimes referred to as the New Zealand ash.

The pre-European Maori found many uses for an oil that was extracted from titoki seeds by pounding.

Crushed aromatic leaves were added to the oil when it was used to anoint the bodies of chiefs. Titoki oil was also used on bruises, for sore ears and to relieve arthritis.

Propagation of titoki is by seed. Seedlings often occur near established trees and these can be transplanted during winter.

ALSEUOSMIA
Apocynaceae

There are five species of *Alseuosmia* native to New Zealand. They are evergreen shrubs, noted for their sweetly scented flowers. One species, *A. macrophylla*, is very showy in bloom but the others have inconspicuous flowers. In nature they are usually found in the interior of forests, and similar conditions of cool, moist shade should be provided for them in gardens. Several species are usually obtainable from specialist native plant nurseries.

Alseuosmia macrophylla
Toropara

A bushy shrub up to two metres high with dark green foliage. In spring it bears beautiful trumpet-shaped flowers, which are deliciously scented. The flower colour varies from dark red to cream. Toropara must have shaded conditions if it is to succeed in cultivation. It also requires a soil that is rich in humus and well drained but does not become dry.

Aphids are sometimes a problem, and at the first sign of infestation appropriate measures should be taken to eradicate this pest.

All species are readily propagated by semi-hardwood cuttings.

ARISTOTELIA
Elaeocarpaceae

The two New Zealand species are endemic. One is a fast-growing tree that is useful as a quick filler until other trees establish. The other is a low-growing shrub. Both species are cold hardy.

Aristotelia fruticosa
Mountain wineberry

A low-growing, small-leaved shrub, which seldom reaches a height of more than one metre. The stiff branches grow close together and are often entangled. Its main attraction is the berries, which occur from late summer until mid-winter. In the best forms they are pink and very showy. Mountain wineberry grows well in an average to moderately rich, well-drained soil. Regular pruning results in a compact shape and is also said to encourage a more prolific crop of berries.

Propagation is by semi-hardwood cuttings, which strike readily.

Aristotelia serrata
Wineberry

Wineberry is one of the commonest native trees, occurring throughout New Zealand. In the wild it is one of those valuable trees that rapidly colonise bare ground and is often the first tree to appear after erosion or fire. Its size makes it unsuitable for small gardens, although it is sometimes used as a quick filler for shelter and to provide light shade for plants requiring such conditions. If it were not for its tendency to be short lived, the wineberry would probably be more popular as a specimen tree in large gardens for it has a graceful, upright to spreading habit of growth and attractive light green foliage. Where winters are cold, the wineberry is completely deciduous. In mild climates some leaves are retained.

The rose-pink flowers of the wineberry are its greatest attraction. They appear in October and November. In the best dark-coloured forms the flowers are very pale when they first open, deepening as they age. This produces an attractive variation in colour between the individual blooms in each bunch of flowers. Male and female flowers occur on separate trees, those of the male tree being larger and more attractive. Both sexes must be grown to produce the small, dark red to almost black berries.

Early settlers used the wood of wineberry trees to make charcoal for gunpowder.

Propagation of the wineberry is by seed or cuttings.

ARTHROPODIUM
Liliaceae

The two species of *Arthropodium* native to New Zealand are endemic. They are both of interest for gardens, especially the versatile *A. cirratum*.

Arthropodium candidum
Star lily

A dainty plant with grass-like leaves and small white flowers, which stand above the foliage on slender, jointed stalks. The best form has coppery bronze foliage. It is a good rock-garden plant, forming small clumps to a height of 15 to 20 centimetres. Dies down in winter.

Propagate by division or seed.

Arthropodium cirratum
Rengarenga, rock lily

A perennial with large, strap-shaped light green, shiny leaves and showy white flowers, which are produced on long stems in December and January. It is by nature a plant of cliff faces near the sea but is surprisingly

adaptable in gardens. It will grow in the open or in shade, in rich or poor soils. The fleshy leaves are easily damaged by frost but this can be overcome by positioning plants beneath the protective canopy of evergreen trees. Slugs and snails can disfigure the leaves too; a few slug pellets around the plants will quickly overcome this problem.

The rock lily grows as high as 70 centimetres, occasionally more in good conditions. It has an attractive form, resembling a tidy, compact-growing, fleshy-leaved flax bush. There are several different forms, some having pure white flowers and others narrow foliage and a more compact habit of growth. This plant is well suited to growing beside a path or at the corner of a building, where its recurved foliage will provide a graceful informality. It also looks striking when grouped in front of shrubs. But possibly the most effective way of using the rock lily is as a massed ground-cover planting beneath tall trees, where its foliage will provide interest all year round and the white flowers will stand out superbly in the low light.

It is simple to propagate by division or from seed, so it is relatively easy to build up a good stock of plants for a massed planting.

Arthropodium cirratum thrives in shade.

A massed planting of *Arthropodium cirratum* beneath tall trees in a Taihape garden.

Astelia chathamica 'Silver Spear'

A hybrid *Astelia* (*A. nervosa* X *chathamica*)

Astelia nervosa

ASTELIA
Liliaceae

Astelias are exciting foliage plants, their spiky leaves in shades of silver, green or bronze providing dramatic effect in the garden. They also make distinctive container plants, and the foliage of the bigger species is useful for floral work.

Propagation is by seed or division.

Astelia chathamica

An outstanding species and usually the easiest to obtain from nurseries. It has bold, silver-green, recurving leaves and looks rather like a silver-foliage flax. (In its native Chatham Islands it is often called Moriori flax.) In time it will form a large clump.

As with all astelias, male and female flowers are borne on separate plants. The orange fruits that follow the flowers on the female plants are highly ornamental.

A. chathamica is an interesting alternative to flax (Phormium). It provides the same bold form yet it is much easier to maintain for it is a tidier grower. The old leaves usually wither away inconspicuously, unlike those of flax, which need to be cut off regularly to keep plants looking tidy. It grows well in an open or slightly shaded situation and adapts well to a variety of soil conditions, although a moderately rich, peaty soil seems to suit it best.

Astelia nervosa

This is one of several Astelia species that vary considerably in the wild, both in the size of plants and foliage colour. Some outstanding forms are available, including some with bronze and silver leaves. A. nervosa has potential for hybridising, and successful results have already been achieved by Felix Jury of Waitara in crossing A. nervosa with A. chathamica.

A. nervosa will grow in sun or shade but the foliage colourings are better when plants are in the open. A well-drained, medium loam seems ideal. Plants should be watered during dry weather.

BEILSCHMIEDIA
Lauraceae

Two species are native to New Zealand. Both are handsome foliage trees suitable for larger gardens.

Beilschmiedia tarairi
Taraire

This tall tree is particularly attractive during its early years when it is very upright in habit with a thin trunk and comparatively few slender branches. Mature specimens have a rounded crown and make good shade trees. The leaves of taraire are large and distinctive, dark shiny green on the upper surface, pale and dull on the underside. A reddish brown velvety covering of hairs is a feature of the flower stalks, branchlets, and the undersides of young leaves. The flowers, produced about December, are small and inconspicuous. They are followed by purple-coloured, oval-shaped fruits up to 3.5 centimetres long, keenly sought after by wood pigeons. The fruits also provided food for the Maori, who steamed the kernels in a hangi for up to two days to make them ready to eat.

B. tarairi is only moderately hardy to frosts. A good, deep, well-drained soil is ideal. It will tolerate quite dry conditions but grows much better if provided with water during periods of drought.

Plants are raised from seed.

Beilschmiedia tawa
Tawa

This tall tree is a common sight in native forests throughout the North Island. It also occurs, but to a lesser extent, in the upper portion of the South Island. It has an erect habit of growth and narrow, pointed leaves. The flowers are tiny and of little interest. The purple-black berries are eaten by wood pigeons and were gathered by the Maori in times gone by for food. Tawa also provided wood for the lengthy (10 metres or more) bird spears of the Maori.

Tawa makes an attractive specimen or background tree for a large garden. It is one of those trees that gains in appeal as it ages and should not be judged prematurely as to its garden worth. It requires similar growing conditions to B. tarairi.

Propagation is by seed.

BRACHYGLOTTIS
Compositae

Until recently the genus Brachyglottis contained only one species, B. repanda, and its several varieties. Recent name changes by botanists have resulted in the genus being enlarged considerably, with many of the plants formerly known as Senecio now being included in Brachyglottis. However, because this book is very much a work for amateurs and because some senecios are well known to gardeners by their old name, we have retained the old nomenclature.

Brachyglottis repanda
Rangiora

A fast-growing, bushy shrub with large and handsome leaves that are light green on top and white underneath. The undersides of the leaves are soft and felt-like and can be written on reasonably easily, to the delight of children; in early times when the settlers were short of note paper these leaves sometimes provided a useful substitute.

Rangiora produces large sprays of cream-coloured flowers in spring. It will reach a height of three metres or more, but can be kept lower by pruning. It will grow in sun or shade, and grows beneath large trees without any problems. Any reasonably well-drained soil should be suitable. Where there are heavy frosts, it requires protection. Stands up well to wind.

Propagate by cuttings.

Brachyglottis repanda 'Purpurea'

The leaves of this striking cultivar are dark purple on top, contrasting strikingly with the silvery white undersides. The size and colour of the foliage makes this an outstanding foliage shrub, particularly useful for providing impact in landscaping. Suitable for growing in large containers. Should be planted in a sunny situation to bring out the deepest foliage colours, otherwise culture is the same as recommended for the species.

BULBINELLA
Liliaceae

Six species of *Bulbinella* are native to New Zealand. They should not be confused with the several species from South Africa, which are sometimes seen in gardens in this country. The native bulbinellas are usually only available from a few specialist native plant nurseries.

Bulbinella hookerii

Bulbinella angustifolia
Maori onion

A bulbous, hardy plant with fleshy green leaves, which grows to a height of 60 centimetres. The foliage dies down in winter. In late spring it has poker-like, golden yellow flowers, which rise up above the foliage. A well-established clump in full flower is a spectacular sight. It is easy to grow if provided with a cool, damp place. Plants resent disturbance and should be planted out in their permanent positions as soon as possible and not transplanted again.

Bulbinella hookeri

This is usually a more robust species than *B. angustifolia*. It has striking yellow flowers and is an attractive and distinctive plant for a rock garden or border. It likes lots of moisture but should have good drainage.

Bulbinellas can be raised from seed.

CAREX
Cyperaceae

A large genus of sedges, containing more than 70 native species. Some are very ornamental and are of considerable interest for gardens, providing striking texture and combining superbly with other plants, particularly shrubs with bold foliage or form or colourful flowers. Most species grow with great ease in widely varying situations, standing up well to wind and proving extremely cold hardy. Any reasonably well-drained soil seems to be suitable. They will grow in full sun or light shade, but the best foliage colours are developed when they are right out in the open. Most of the species in cultivation make good ground-cover plants, looking especially effective when used to cover banks. The dense foliage prevents most weeds from gaining a foothold.

Carex are easily increased by division in winter. They can also be raised from seed.

Carex buchananii

An erect, robust species with reddish brown foliage. Grows to a height of 60 centimetres. A good plant for contrast in a large rock garden or in front of shrubs with distinctive foliage.

Carex flagellifera

An interesting species, more upright in habit than *C. lucida*. Has long, arching, brown foliage, which sways with the wind in a graceful fashion. If planted next to shrubs with bold foliage, such as flaxes, it makes a charming contrast. Very hardy and easy to grow. Its pretty seed-heads on long slender stalks can be used in dried-flower arrangements.

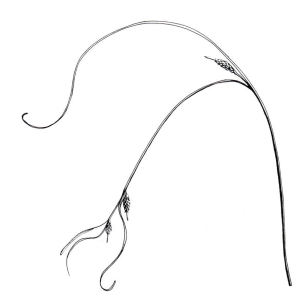

Seed-heads of *Carex flagellifera*.

Carex lucida

A beautiful species with long, wavy, cascading strands of shiny copper-coloured foliage. It grows to a height of 20 centimetres or so and provides interest wherever it is planted. Makes a good ground cover and combines well with colourful shrubs. Also a good companion plant for ornamental native grasses such as *Chionochloa flavicans* and *Cortaderia richardii*. Looks superb in a large group on a bank, or cascading from a tall, slim planter, and is a marvellous plant for imaginative and low-maintenance landscaping projects. Easy to grow.

Carex lucida

CARMICHAELIA
Papilionaceae

There are 39 species of *Carmichaelia* native to New Zealand. The only remaining species in the genus occurs on Lord Howe Island. They range in size from tiny, ground-hugging shrubs to small trees six metres or more in height. Most species, with the notable exception of *C. williamsii*, have small, white, pea-like flowers veined with purple. The majority of species also share the distinctive characteristic of being leafless, the green branchlets functioning as leaves. Although many species are insignificant, there are some that make attractive and distinctive garden plants. They will tolerate poor soils and dry conditions but perform much better if planted in an average to moderately rich, reasonably well-drained soil and provided with moisture during prolonged periods of dry weather. All species except *C. williamsii* are completely cold hardy.

Carmichaelia cunninghamii

This free-flowering shrub produces small purple blooms thickly on the branchlets in early summer. It will grow to a height of three metres and varies in its habit of growth. Some forms have weeping branches, which makes them particularly attractive.

Carmichaelia grandiflora

A much-branched shrub up to two metres high. The cream or lilac flowers are pleasantly scented and the weeping foliage is also a pleasing characteristic. This worthwhile garden plant grows best in good soil, although it will tolerate quite poor and dry conditions.

Carmichaelia odorata

This is an attractive, much-branched shrub with weeping branchlets and scented white flowers mottled with purple. Flowering time is from early to mid-summer. This species grows to a height of about two metres and usually has small leaves on the flattened branchlets during spring and summer. It is worth growing for both the scented flowers and the pleasing pendulous habit.

Carmichaelia williamsii

This is the most distinctive species of *Carmichaelia*, having broad, very flat stems and large yellow flowers with purple veining. It is an interesting shrub, for both its flowers and its form. The flowers hang in small bunches from the leafless stems and make an attractive though not spectacular display. The plant in my garden blooms freely from early to late winter and is much appreciated at that time of year.

As a shrub for landscaping use, *C. williamsii* has a most interesting form. The flat, often twisting and

Carmichaelia williamsii

sometimes weeping branchlets and the absence of leaves make this shrub stand out from most others. If it is used in association with other natives with bold or unusual foliage — for example, *Pseudopanax ferox, Griselinia lucida, Astelia chathamica,* or *Phormium* — the effect can be dramatic.

C. williamsii usually grows to a height of two metres in cultivation and has a tidy, compact habit. It may not be quite as hardy to cold as other species, although it should have no difficulty growing in most lowland districts. It seems to grow and flower with equal ease in full sun or light shade.

In nature it occurs on the Poor Knights, Little Barrier and Alderman Islands and in coastal areas from the Bay of Plenty to East Cape.

All species of *Carmichaelia* can be propagated by cuttings.

CARPODETUS
Escalloniaceae

The only native species, a small to medium-sized tree, is endemic.

Carpodetus serratus
Putaputaweta

This is an attractive tree, seldom higher than five to six metres in cultivation, with spreading branches arranged in a tier-like pattern. It is suitable for growing as an individual specimen or background tree or for including in a mixed planting of trees and shrubs.

The pale creamy grey bark and the dark green, leathery, marbled foliage are distinctive. The white flowers, which occur from early to late summer, are small but are produced in great numbers.

Putaputaweta will grow in most soil types, but a deep, reasonably rich soil is preferred. In poor or dry soils it grows slowly and does not produce its best form, but in good conditions growth is quite rapid. It is hardy to cold but requires shelter from wind in exposed situations.

Putaputaweta undergoes a juvenile stage in which the leaves are small and the habit of growth is rather straggly, with spreading, interlacing branchlets. This juvenile form can be bypassed by propagating plants from cuttings taken from adult trees.

CASSINIA
Compositae

There are five native species, all of which are endemic. They are fast-growing shrubs, particularly useful in poor, dry soils, where they establish easily. Good for providing quick shelter for slower-growing shrubs and trees. Generally they are not highly regarded as ornamentals, although one species at least, *C. fulvida,* deserves a better reputation. All species are improved by a once-yearly pruning after flowering.

They are easily propagated from cuttings.

Cassinia fulvida
Golden tauhinu, golden cottonwood

A bushy, much-branched, hardy shrub up to two metres high, with golden yellow stems and leaves, the colouring being most pronounced when it is grown in an exposed, sunny situation and a poor, dry soil. Regular clipping will encourage a compact shape. A good shrub for beach gardens. *C. fulvida* var. *montana* has small, bright green foliage, white flowers that are far more conspicuous than those of the species, and a more compact habit of growth.

Cassinia fulvida var. *montana*

CELMISIA
Compositae

Celmisias, or mountain daisies as they are well known, are beautiful plants with white daisy-like flowers that occur in summer. Most *Celmisia* species grow in the wild in alpine regions but a few occur at low altitudes. In cultivation they are usually grown in rock gardens, where their natural conditions can be duplicated to some degree. They like to grow in the crevices between rocks and to have a light, gritty material such as fine gravel on the upper surface. The roots should be able to reach a lower level where the soil is heavier and more moisture retentive than the surface layer.

Celmisias often prove difficult where the summers are hot and humid. They are at their best in inland gardens and in the South Island, where the atmosphere is clear and the winters are cold.

Celmisias can be obtained from nurseries specialising in native plants. They can also be raised from seed.

CHIONOCHLOA
Gramineae

Most *Chionochloa* species are found in alpine regions. They are the well-known snow tussocks or snow-grasses that form a conspicuous part of the low alpine flora. However, the most significant species for gardens, *C. flavicans*, occurs only in warm lowland areas of the North Island.

Chionochloa flavicans

This handsome tussock is one of the most ornamental of the many outstanding native grasses suitable for gardens. It forms dense clumps up to one metre high by 1.5 metres wide. The bright green leaves are long, slender and weeping, and during mid-summer beautiful plumes of greenish yellow flowers hang from the tips of metre-long stems. The flowers last for a surprisingly long time and are popular for floral work. The graceful appearance of *C. flavicans* makes it useful for numerous situations in gardens, and its weeping habit makes it a natural choice for planting beside water or to cascade over a low wall. It is also striking in a large rock garden or in a big planter of the type often used in public landscaping projects.

It combines particularly well with bronze-leaved native grasses such as some of the *Carex* species and can also look effective when grown among native or exotic shrubs. Where space permits, it can be planted in a big drift in front of trees or used as a weed-suppressing massed planting on a bank.

C. flavicans will grow readily in any average, well-drained garden soil. Poor soils can be made more suitable by incorporating organic matter such as compost or peat prior to planting. Full sun or dappled shade suit it equally well. It seems to be hardy to cold in most lowland districts.

The simplest method of propagation is division of established plants. The best time for this operation is autumn. Plants can also be raised from seed.

Chionochloa flavicans

CHORDOSPARTIUM
Papilionaceae

There is only one species belonging to the genus *Chordospartium*. It is a highly distinctive, small, leafless tree with great possibilities for landscaping, yet it remains little appreciated by most gardeners.

Chordospartium stevensonii
Weeping broom, tree broom

This small tree develops great character as it matures. When established, it displays an upright habit, a distinctive greenish bark and an umbrella-like crown of slender, weeping, leafless branchlets. Masses of pale lavender flowers cover the branchlets in December and January, lasting for about three weeks. In cultivation the weeping broom seldom reaches a height of more than four metres, although trees twice this height do occur in the wild. It makes a most distinctive specimen tree and its compact size makes it suitable for planting in small gardens. It can look superb in association with modern architecture and is ideal for the style of landscaping that concentrates on form, texture and contrast for impact rather than relying solely on bright colour. But wherever the weeping broom is planted, it should be allowed to stand on its own; when placed among other shrubs and trees its unusual form has far less impact.

C. stevensonii looks rather insignificant during its early years, which may explain to some extent why it is not more popular with gardeners. However, its striking mature form is ample reward for putting up with its unimposing appearance while young. Although it will grow in rather poor and dry conditions, the rate of growth is greatly improved if it is planted in a good garden soil, preferably in a sunny situation. It is very hardy to cold.

The natural habitat of *C. stevensonii* is alluvial river flats in inland Marlborough, where it is found alongside tributaries of the Awatere, Clarence and Wairau Rivers, between 450 and 750 metres altitude. In *The Cultivation of New Zealand Trees and Shrubs* (Reed), Metcalf points out that there is some variation among wild forms and adds: 'Before it becomes too widely cultivated it would be wise to make sure the best form is selected.'

Propagation is by seed. To encourage germination, the hard seed surface can be chipped with a knife or the seeds can be briefly immersed in boiling water then soaked in cold water for a day before sowing. Cuttings are usually difficult to strike.

If plants cannot be purchased from local plant retailers, consult the mail-order lists of nurseries specialising in native plants.

CLADIUM
Cyperaceae

The one species native to New Zealand is an interesting, easily grown but little-known plant, which could be used more often in modern landscaping.

Cladium sinclairii

When not in flower, *C. sinclairii* attracts little attention with its broad, strap-like green leaves up to one metre long. But in spring, when the long-stemmed heads

Cladium sinclairii

of shaggy, rusty brown flowers are present in great numbers, this plant is most attractive and very distinctive. The weeping flowers, which hang from the ends of the slender, recurving stems, look striking beside water. This species fits in well with planting schemes featuring foliage plants such as native grasses, astelias and flaxes. It also combines well with stones and can serve as an interesting contrast to shrubs. When established, it forms a clump up to 60 centimetres in diameter.

In the wild, *C. sinclairii* is usually found on damp cliff-sides near the coast and up to a height of 400 metres, from North Cape to about Wanganui. In cultivation it grows with ease in any average garden soil, in full sun or light shade, and seems to be cold hardy. Plants are often hard to obtain from nurseries, although some of those specialising in native plants include it in their mail-order lists.

Plants can be increased by dividing established clumps (each rooted piece will grow), or by seed.

CLEMATIS
Ranunculaceae

There are approximately 10 species of *Clematis* native to New Zealand. One species, the rare *C. marmoraria*, is a dwarf shrub; the others are climbers. Most have rather insignificant flowers but several are showy and are definitely worthwhile in gardens. One species in particular, *C. paniculata*, is outstanding and is sought after in some overseas countries as well as being very popular in its country of origin. Most other species are not readily available, although some of the specialist native plant nurseries may be a source of supply. Clematis should be planted in a situation where the roots can enjoy cool shade but the vine can grow into the sun to flower.

Native *Clematis* species bear male and female flowers on separate plants. Because the male flowers are usually bigger and more attractive, it is the male plants that are the most desired by gardeners. To be sure of obtaining male clematis vines, semi-hardwood or hardwood cuttings should be struck. Seedlings will, of course, be either male or female and there will be no indication of the sex until they flower.

Clematis paniculata
Puawhananga

To see a well-established specimen of this clematis in full flower is always a thrill. In the New Zealand bush it is often seen growing through the tops of trees, making a large patch of glistening white flowers in spring. It will grow in a similar manner in gardens, climbing to the top of an evergreen tree or over a support such as trellis. It can look particularly attractive growing through a deciduous tree such as a silver birch, draping the branches with its slender, dark green foliage and usually producing its stunning

Clematis paniculata growing on a rimu (*Dacrydium cupressinum*).

flowers before the new leaves develop in spring.

If seedling plants of *C. paniculata* are grown, they go through several juvenile stages before they start to flower. Plants grown from cuttings taken from mature vines do not undergo the juvenile-foliage stage and flower prolifically from an early age.

CLIANTHUS
Papilionaceae

Only one species occurs in New Zealand. It is among the rarest of native plants in the wild but, thankfully, its popularity ensures its preservation in gardens. It is interesting to note that *Clianthus* was one of the few ornamental plants cultivated by the pre-European Maori, who held the beautiful flowers in high regard.

Clianthus puniceus
Kaka beak, kowhai-ngutu-kaka

Kaka beak is a favourite in gardens throughout New Zealand. It forms a shrub 1.5 to two metres high, with spreading branches thickly clothed with light green, fine foliage. The showy flowers are beautifully formed, looking very much like upside-down parrots'

beaks. The flowers hang in clusters from the branches, and a well-grown plant can be covered with blooms. The peak flowering is in spring, but the season often extends for many months, starting in winter.

The flower colour varies. Three colour forms are readily available: red, pink, and white. All are most attractive, the red usually proving the most popular. A light pruning after flowering will encourage even more prolific blooming and a compact habit of growth.

Kaka beak is easy to grow in most soils providing there is good drainage. Once established, it will tolerate dry conditions. A sunny situation will encourage the greatest number of flowers. Kaka beak is an excellent choice for a mixed shrub border and can also be trained to grow close against a wall. It is usually quite hardy to cold, although very young plants may suffer some damage from heavy frosts.

Unfortunately, kaka beak tends to be short lived, but it is such an attractive shrub that it is well worth replanting if the need arises. Plants are often attacked by a leaf-miner, which burrows into the leaves. This is easily controlled by spraying if the infestation is severe, but often the problem is slight and can be safely ignored. A more serious problem is a witches' broom, which causes deformed, gall-like growths and should be pruned off when first seen.

Clianthus puniceus

Propagation is by seed or cuttings — either method is easy — but good colour forms should be raised from cuttings to ensure their characteristics are retained.

'Witches brooms', caused by infestations of mites, sometimes occur on *Clianthus*. They should be cut off when they first appear.

COPROSMA
Rubiaceae

Fifty species of *Coprosma* are native to New Zealand. They range in size from small trees to prostrate plants suitable for rock gardens. Some are superb coastal plants; others are among the most outstanding foliage shrubs and are widely used in landscaping. They respond well to clipping and can be kept to a desired size or shape by this means; old plants that have become leggy can be rejuvenated by hard cutting back. Many coprosmas have brightly coloured berries, but it must be remembered that most species have male and female flowers on separate plants and unless both sexes are present it is unlikely that berries will be produced. In addition to the species, there are a number of cultivars and hybrids, and new ones are steadily becoming available. The following list is limited to those that are usually available from nurseries and are well suited to gardens.

Clianthus puniceus 'Roseus'

Clianthus puniceus foliage is sometimes attacked by a leaf miner.

Coprosma acerosa
Sand coprosma

This extremely hardy plant forms low, dense cushions of thin, wiry stems. The green leaves are one centimetre long, extremely thin and spaced well apart, giving the plant a twiggy appearance. Providing there is a male plant present, female plants will produce shiny berries, which are a delightful shade of blue in the best forms. The sand coprosma is ideally suited to poor, dryish soils and full sun. In better soils it tends to be less compact. A good candidate for beach gardens and for sunny banks, it grows easily and is readily propagated by cuttings.

Coprosma australis
Kanono

A tall-growing species with large, shiny, green leaves and large clusters of colourful berries. It is useful for

Coprosma acerosa

shelter and for growing in difficult shaded conditions such as beneath large trees where the soil is dry and few plants will succeed.

Coprosma 'Beatson's Gold'

A small, bushy shrub that grows to a height of approximately one metre. The small leaves are golden yellow edged with green. It is attractive in front of taller shrubs, among other compact shrubs, and in combination with green and bronze foliage. It is hardy and grows with ease, and should have an open, sunny situation.

Propagate from cuttings.

Coprosma brunnea X 'Kirkii'

A prostrate, mat-forming, tiny-leaved shrub, which is superb for banks and walls and is also a good, weed-suppressing ground cover. The brownish green, close-knit foliage will cascade straight down a sheer wall, in similar fashion to prostrate rosemary. Makes an interesting contrast in texture when used as a cover plant among low shrubs. It likes an open, sunny situation and well-drained soil, but is hardy and grows with ease in poor, dry soils.

Propagate by cuttings.

Coprosma 'Coppershine'

A bushy, upright shrub, seldom higher than two metres. The shiny green leaves are shaded brown around the margins. It is a handsome garden shrub and it also makes a distinctive hedge. It should have an open sunny situation. Will grow easily in most soil types, is hardy to cold and wind, and is drought tolerant.

Coprosma 'Kirkii'

A tough, wide-spreading ground cover, which has been popular for many years. It has olive-green, narrow leaves and a dense habit of growth, which helps to suppress weeds. It is a good plant for beach gardens, growing with ease in poor, dry, sandy soils, yet it is also perfectly happy in moderately rich soils with good drainage. An excellent plant for banks and for covering large areas, it has its uses in public landscaping as well as in the home garden. Makes a good foreground plant for shrubs with colourful foliage, such as flaxes. Can be clipped to keep it to a desired size or shape.

Easily propagated by cuttings.

Coprosma 'Kirkii' covering a low bank in front of *Metrosideros kermadecensis* 'Variegata', the variegated Kermadec pohutukawa.

Coprosma 'Kirkii Variegata'

This plant has green and cream variegated leaves, otherwise it is the same as C. 'Kirkii'. A striking ground cover, it combines particularly well with dark green foliage.

Coprosma 'Kiwi Gold'

Similar in habit to C. 'Prostrata' but slower growing. The leaves are prominently marked with gold, with

Coprosma 'Kirkii Variegata'

Coprosma 'Kiwi Gold'

Coprosma 'Prostrata'

a dark green margin. It is a handsome ground cover or bank plant, spreading up to one metre. Will grow in any well-drained soil and withstands dry conditions. It is best in full sun; in shade it tends to develop a straggly habit of growth.

Propagation is by cuttings, which are easy to strike.

Coprosma 'Prostrata'

A low-growing or prostrate shrub suitable for ground cover and for banks and walls. The stems of dark, shiny, green foliage will cascade several metres down a wall in dramatic fashion. It is suitable for gardens

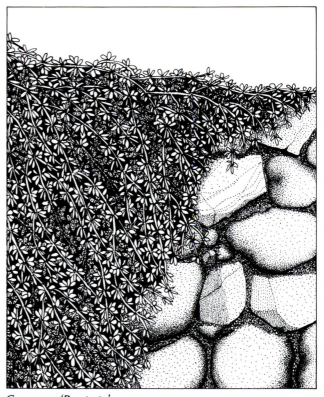

Coprosma 'Prostrata'

near the sea, standing up well to salt winds and thriving in poor, dry soils. Also grows well in reasonably rich soils providing there is good drainage and an open, sunny situation. Makes a thick mat of foliage that smothers weeds.

Propagate by cuttings, which strike readily.

Coprosma repens
Taupata

Taupata is a coastal plant by nature and is capable of growing in extremely barren and windswept coastal sites where few other shrubs could survive. In such exposed situations it is often low growing, even prostrate at times, but in more sheltered conditions it is of upright habit, growing to a height of five metres or more. Taupata is easily distinguished by its thick and glossy, broadly oblong, dark green leaves, which roll back at the edges and have a prominent mid-vein.

This is an outstanding plant for exposed situations. It makes a good hedge or shelter plant, growing easily in poor, dry soils, although it will also grow in quite rich soils. Its main requirements are good drainage and a sunny situation. Although it is usually disregarded as an ornamental, it makes an attractive background shrub and can be an effective foil to variegated and brightly coloured foliage. Taupata is hardy to cold in most lowland districts.

Propagation is by cuttings or seed.

Coprosma repens

Coprosma repens 'Variegata'

Coprosma repens 'Picturata'

A handsome cultivar that has irregular bright yellow to green-yellow variegations and a broad margin of dark green. It forms a large, bushy shrub, which can be clipped to shape if desired or allowed to assume its natural form. It makes an attractive hedge and can also be trained to grow against a wall. Cultural requirements are the same as for *C. repens*.

Propagation is by cuttings.

Coprosma repens 'Silver Queen'

The leaves of this cultivar have mottled green and white markings. It is a colourful shrub with a bushy habit of growth and makes an interesting contrast to bold-foliage shrubs and trees such as *Meryta sinclairii*. It can also look striking as a massed group in front of taller, green-leaved shrubs and trees. If clipped regularly, it makes a distinctive hedge.

Can be propagated by cuttings.

Coprosma repens 'Variegata'

The leaves of this cultivar have a broad margin of creamy yellow with an irregular blotch of medium green in the centre. The overall foliage colouring is much lighter than that of *C. repens* 'Picturata'. It is a delightful foliage shrub with many possibilities in landscaping. The habit of growth is often looser and more spreading than the other cultivars, making it most useful as a bank plant or to soften the corner of a building or the edge of a driveway. It combines well with bronze-foliage native grasses and makes a delightful contrast in form at the base of a very upright tree such as *Cordyline australis*. Cultural requirements as for *C. repens*.

Propagate by cuttings.

Coprosma robusta
Karamu

A large shrub or small tree three to four metres high, with dark green, shiny leaves. It often produces

A mixed planting of *Coprosma repens* 'Variegata', *C. repens* 'Silver Queen' and *C. repens* 'Picturata'

prolific crops of orange berries, which make a great show. The rate of growth is quite rapid and it is very hardy to wind, making it useful for quick shelter. It grows readily in sun or shade and is capable of doing well under tall trees. Regular trimming will help to keep it bushy.

Plants can be propagated from cuttings or seed.

Coprosma robusta 'Williamsii Variegata'

The leaves of this cultivar display attractive pale green, dark green and creamy green variegations surrounded by an irregular cream margin. This is a magnificent foliage shrub for a shaded situation. It will grow in the open but the white portion of the leaves tends to burn in full sun. In shade the pale foliage shows up to perfection. It is a bushy shrub, usually no more than one metre in height, although I have seen specimens a good two metres tall trained against shaded walls. The pale foliage can lighten up a sombre shaded area most effectively and is striking when used as a contrast among green-leaved shrubs. It can be trained to grow close against a wall by pruning the outward-facing growths a little.

Coprosma williamsii 'Variegata' grows readily in most soil types. It requires protection from heavy frosts.

Propagation is by cuttings of firm tip growths.

Coprosma robusta 'Williamsii Variegata'

CORDYLINE
Agavaceae

The five species of *Cordyline* native to New Zealand are endemic. They are excellent for landscaping, providing a distinctive tropical appearance. The well-known cabbage tree, *C. australis*, is remarkably adaptable and its coloured and variegated foliage forms make it one of the most notable of native foliage trees.

Cordyline australis
Cabbage tree, ti kouka

This remarkable tree is a feature of the New Zealand landscape. Its palm-like appearance seems tropical yet it is hardy to cold. The cabbage tree grows with ease in widely varying situations, from poor, windswept hillsides near the sea to swamps far inland. In private and public gardens it provides a definite New Zealand character, which is often a welcome change from the ubiquitous English garden look. Its bold form can be used to create a focal point and as a contrast to rounded plant forms. If several specimens are planted in a group, the result is most pleasing. Cabbage trees are striking when used to line a driveway, and they also make highly ornamental street trees and are well suited to growing in containers.

The cabbage tree is grown primarily for its form but the flowers are a great attraction too. In November and December established trees are usually covered with large panicles of creamy white, scented flowers.

One disadvantage of cabbage trees is that the old leaves fall throughout the year. They are tough and stringy, and cause difficulties with mowers if they become entangled in the blades, but such problems can be overcome by positioning cabbage trees among other trees and shrubs some distance away from lawns.

The usual method of propagation is from seed, but plants can also be grown from cuttings.

Cordyline australis 'Albertii'

This beautiful cultivar has cream and green variegated foliage, with a pink mid-rib that adds a gorgeous flush of colour to the new growth. Despite the tropical appearance, it is quite hardy and grows with ease in most soil types and situations. It looks marvellous when positioned so the foliage is viewed against the light. It is striking as a container plant but should be planted in a rich soil mix and given regular applications of fertiliser when grown in this manner. The foliage is sometimes damaged by chewing insects; keep a careful watch in summer and take the appropriate control measures at the first sign of problems.

Propagation of this cultivar is only possible by vegetative means, usually cuttings.

Cordyline australis 'Purpurea'

This cultivar differs from the species only in its foliage colouring, which varies from bronze to purple. The

Cordyline australis

Cordyline australis 'Albertii'

purple-leaved forms are the most desirable. A more dramatic tree than the species, it could be used far more in gardens than it is at present.

Cordyline banksii
Ti ngahere, forest cabbage tree

This attractive species is not nearly as well known as *C. australis* but in many respects it is better suited for garden use, especially where space is limited. It often branches from the base, forming flax-like clumps of thin, pale green, drooping foliage. The strongly scented flowers are the whitest and showiest of the native *Cordyline* species. Ti ngahere grows best in a good soil.

It can be raised from seed.

Cordyline banksii 'Purpurea'

The leaves of this cultivar are bronze-purple, but apart from this it is the same as the species. It is very handsome but seems to have been largely displaced in recent years by *C. australis* 'Purpurea'.

It can be raised from seed as a large proportion of the seedlings usually have the same foliage colour.

Cordyline indivisa
Toii, broad-leaved or mountain cabbage tree

This is the most handsome cabbage tree, its broad leaves, bold reddish mid-rib and large head making it stand out in any company. It develops on a single trunk, reaching a height of seven to eight metres. The creamy white flowers are borne in large, pendulous panicles. A beautiful subject for contrast among shrubs with fine foliage or as a focal point among native tussock grasses.

Toii is by nature a tree of high country where there is steady rainfall and cool, often misty conditions. In gardens it can prove difficult where the summers are hot and dry but usually grows well in districts such as Taranaki where there is reliable rainfall all year round. A cool situation and a deep, rich soil are essential.

Plants can be raised from seed.

Cordyline kaspar
Three Kings cabbage tree

Found in the wild only on the Three Kings Islands, this handsome species has shorter and wider leaves than *C. australis* and it grows to a lesser height, has far more branches and a much stouter appearance. It is a delightful tree for gardens, having an elegant form, seldom growing to a height of more than three metres, and producing perfumed flowers freely. Well worth growing as a solitary specimen in a prominent position. It grows with ease in most soil types but is liable to damage by heavy frosts, especially in its first few years.

Cordyline pumilio
Ti koraha, dwarf cabbage tree

This dwarf species looks more like a grass than a cabbage tree. It grows to a height of slightly less than one metre and has thin, brown leaves. The widely spaced, scented flowers are produced from November to January. It is of interest for a rock garden or in front of shrubs and is also suitable for growing in a container. Plant in an open, sunny situation. A deep, moderately rich, well-drained soil is ideal. Hardy to cold in most districts.

Cordyline indivisa

Cordyline kaspar

COROKIA
Cornaceae

With the exception of one species, *C. buddleioides*, corokias are tough shrubs that thrive in dry soils and windswept situations. In beach gardens and on bleak hillsides they are hard to beat for reliability and for an attractive display of flowers and berries. Corokias all have masses of small, star-shaped, bright yellow flowers that cover the bushes in spring, and most have a good display of red, orange or yellow berries from autumn until well into winter. Corokias are used extensively for hedging, particularly *C. cotoneaster* and most of the hybrids, which are long lived and extremely tough. They can be trimmed to form a very narrow or low hedge if desired. Where greater height is wanted, they will make a two-metre-high wall of foliage. The close, interlacing pattern of growth of corokias such as *C. cotoneaster* makes for an extremely neat hedge if clipped regularly. Corokias are cold hardy.

Corokias are usually propagated by cuttings, which strike easily. They can be raised from seed too, but vegetative propagation is the only means of ensuring that the characteristics of the hybrids are retained.

Corokia buddleioides

A distinctive species, deserving of a place in the shrub border for its attractive foliage and pretty yellow flowers. The long, narrow leaves are pale green, often displaying pretty bronze tints. *C. buddleioides* will grow in light shade, although the foliage colour is better in sun. This species is not as tough as other corokias and should be treated as an ornamental rather than a hardy shelter plant. It forms a bushy shrub two to three metres high.

Corokia buddleioides

Corokia cotoneaster

This shrub is really quite ornamental, despite its reputation as merely a hedging plant. It has a rather twisted and interlaced pattern of growth, dark-coloured bark and small, grey-green leaves with white undersides. The flower display is delightful — the bush is a mass of yellow blooms. If allowed to grow in its natural form, *C. cotoneaster* develops into a rounded bush two metres or so high. It is hardy to salt winds.

Corokia cotoneaster clipped to form a rounded shrub

Corokia macrocarpa

Corokia macrocarpa

A native of the Chatham Islands, *C. macrocarpa* forms an erect, slightly rounded shrub three metres high or more. The green leaves are an attractive feature and it has a showy flower display followed by small, round berries, which are usually bright orange. It is suitable for growing in the dry conditions often encountered beneath large trees as well as in the open.

Corokia X *virgata* 'Cheesemanii'

A handsome shrub that is not as densely branched as *C. cotoneaster*. In spring it has bright yellow flowers, which completely cover the bush, and these are followed by red berries, which remain for a long period. Usually grows to a height of two to three metres.

Cortaderia richardii

Corokia X *virgata* 'Cheesemanii'

CORTADERIA
Gramineae

There are four species of *Cortaderia* native to New Zealand. They are all tall, tussocky grasses with thin, sharp-edged, drooping foliage and plume-like flower-heads on long stems. The common name of toetoe is applied to them all. In addition to the natives there are two South American species that have become widespread in New Zealand. *C. selloana*, the true pampas grass, a native of Argentina, is a common sight throughout the land. It can be distinguished because its flowering time (mid-March to the end of April) is different from that of the native species, all of which produce their flowers at various times from mid-November to January. The other introduced species that has naturalised is *C. jubata*, a native of Peru. It has purplish plumes and is a nuisance in some districts, particularly around Auckland. Among the native toetoes, one species, the elegant *C. richardii*, stands out as an ornamental and is often the only one offered for sale. At times it is difficult to obtain, but most nurseries specialising in native plants can supply it.

Cortaderia richardii
South Island toetoe

This graceful grass produces its large, creamy-coloured, recurved plumes on thin, three-metre-high stems from the middle of December into January. It is a hardy, easily grown plant and can be used in many different situations. Most soil types are suitable, and it will grow in full sun or where sun is received for at least half the day. It looks especially striking among other native grasses such as *Chionochloa flavicans*, *Carex* species and *Festuca coxii*. An assortment of native grasses of this type is an interesting way of planting a bank or creating a natural look and allowing easy maintenance.

Propagation is by seed or division.

CORYNOCARPUS
Corynocarpaceae

One species only — a fast-growing, tall tree — occurs in New Zealand. It is best suited to large gardens; for small gardens, the cultivars with variegated foliage are worth considering.

Corynocarpus laevigatus berries

Corynocarpus laevigatus
Karaka

Karaka made such an impression on Alan Cunningham, an early New Zealand botanist, that he was moved to write about it as 'a tree upon which the eye of the traveller rests with pleasure by reason of its rich dark glossy leaves and highly ornamental growth.' He could have added that its dense, rounded canopy of foliage, sturdy trunk and thick branches are other notable and pleasing features of this striking tree.

A mature karaka will seldom exceed a height of 15 metres, although one exceptional specimen, considered to be the largest in the country, was almost 20 metres when last measured. During spring karaka trees produce small, greenish cream flowers at the ends of the branches. These are followed by large berries, which are shiny green at first and turn bright orange when they ripen about February. The berries, which are a favourite food of the native pigeon, hang in big bunches and make a great show.

The colourful berries produce a slightly unpleasant odour when they fall to the ground and rot beneath the trees. Largely because of this, the karaka is not favoured for planting close to dwellings, but as a background tree for large gardens or as a grove in a farm paddock, it is most attractive. The karaka is also useful as a shelter tree because it stands up well to coastal winds, and it will form a tall, dense hedge if trimmed regularly.

Although the orange flesh of the karaka fruit is edible, the inner seed is highly poisonous in its raw state. For safety's sake, children should be warned that the berries are not to be touched. To the pre-European Maori, the seeds of the karaka were a valued source of food, but before they were rendered edible an involved process of cooking, washing and sun-drying took place. Karaka trees were among the few plants cultivated by the Maori and wherever there were pa sites groves of karaka abounded.

The karaka is by nature a tree of the coast, occurring near the sea over much of the North Island, in parts of the upper South Island and on the Chatham Islands. On the Chathams it is called kopi instead of karaka. Wherever it grows undisturbed, it usually occurs in groves rather than as solitary trees.

A reasonably rich soil is ideal for the karaka, although it will grow in poor soils. Once established, it is tolerant of considerable drought and neglect, but young trees will benefit from watering during extended dry spells. Protection from frost is necessary for young karakas; light to moderate frosts are tolerated by mature trees.

Propagation of karaka is by seed in the case of the species. Fresh seed germinates rapidly, but although masses of seedlings usually occur beneath established trees, even very young trees do not transplant readily because they have long tap roots. The seed should therefore be sown directly into pots or scattered where trees are desired, then lightly covered. The variegated-foliage cultivars must be propagated by cuttings, which is the usual method, or by grafting.

Variegated-foliage cultivars

The following three karakas with variegated foliage are all of interest for the garden. They are slower growing than the green-leaved species and are easier to accommodate in smaller gardens. The variegated karakas are also of interest for growing in containers.

Corynocarpus laevigatus 'Variegatus'

Corynocarpus laevigatus 'Alba Variegatus'

The leaves of this attractive cultivar have a narrow white margin.

Corynocarpus laevigatus 'Picturata'

The dark green leaves have a bold central splash of yellow. It has not been available for nearly as long as the other two cultivars but already it is widely regarded as the most appealing.

Corynocarpus laevigatus 'Variegatus'

This cultivar has been popular for years. The leaves display a wide margin of golden yellow.

COTULA
Compositae

Twenty-four *Cotula* species are native to New Zealand. Most are mat or turf plants and a few species could be considered as alternatives to lawns. Some, such as *C. squalida*, are invasive and should be regarded with suspicion in the garden, but others are delightful plants for the rockery. They are hardy to cold.

Cotula atrata

This is a choice alpine plant that is rather difficult to grow but is so attractive that it is worth repeated attempts in a rock garden. The flowers are dark purple or almost black with golden yellow stamens, and a plant that is growing happily will flower over a very long period.

It is found naturally on rock screes in the mountains of the lower half of the South Island so it is little wonder that it often proves difficult to keep alive in humid, lowland gardens. Excellent drainage is essential; Cartman (*Growing New Zealand Alpine Plants*) recommends that the growing medium should contain 75 per cent stone chips.

Propagation is by seed or cuttings.

Cotula goyenii

This unusual alpine mat plant forms little cushions of apple-green foliage and has tiny purple flowers in spring. It is not difficult to grow providing it has a sunny spot and a well-drained, rather poor soil. If planted in a rich soil, its growth becomes less compact and the charm of the plant is reduced. A good plant to tuck into a crevice in a rock garden.

Easily propagated by cuttings.

Cotula perpusilla

A mat-forming plant with tiny fern-like foliage, which is purple-green in spring and summer, fading to green in winter. Makes a good ground cover for growing around small alpine plants or to cover small bulbs. It is an easy plant to grow in a well-drained but not dry soil. Prefers partial shade.

Propagate by removing rooted pieces.

CYATHODES
Epacridaceae

The genus *Cyathodes* has recently undergone reclassification and some species have been placed back in the genus *Leucopogon*. The two species mentioned here are both attractive shrubs that deserve to be far better known. At present they are seldom seen in gardens.

Cyathodes juniperina

This species is of interest to gardeners mainly because of its attractive fruits, which make a great show. The colour of these varies from white to pink, red to purplish red. The yellow-green leaves are very narrow and sharply pointed, and the stems are a dark brownish black. *C. juniperina* is hardy to cold. A well-

Cyathodes juniperina

drained, rather light soil is ideal, and a reasonably sunny situation is preferred. Once established, it is hardy to cold. The habit of growth is quite erect and the eventual height is usually no more than one to 1.5 metres, although there are some forms that are taller growing. (In the wild there is considerable variation in height between plants in different localities.) It can be kept to a desired height by a little pruning. The natural distribution of this species is in lowland forests over much of New Zealand.

Propagation is usually by seed. It can also be grown from cuttings but these sometimes prove difficult to strike.

Cyathodes robusta
Chatham Island mingimingi

The Chatham Island species is similar to *C. juniperina* but has larger foliage and fruits and is a more robust, taller shrub. It is also more showy, the red-fruited forms being particularly attractive. On the Chatham Islands it is a prominent plant of open scrubland. It requires the same growing conditions as *C. juniperina*.

Plants can be obtained from some of the specialist native plant nurseries.

Cyathodes robusta

DACRYDIUM
Podocarpaceae

There are seven species native to New Zealand, all of which are endemic. Most are of interest for gardens, yet only the magnificent rimu, *Dacrydium cupressinum*, is at all well known and even it is often overlooked in spite of its outstanding qualities.

Propagation of *Dacrydium* species is usually by seed or semi-hardwood cuttings. Cuttings often take some time to produce roots.

Dacrydium bidwillii
Bog pine

A small, slow-growing shrub, which seldom exceeds 1.5 metres in cultivation. It has distinct juvenile and adult foliage, the former being thick and leathery, the latter small, scale-like, overlapping and pressed flat against the stems. *D. bidwillii* is suitable for a large rock garden or the foreground of a shrub border. It responds well to clipping if a more compact shape is desired. Plant in a reasonably rich, not too dry soil and keep it well watered during periods of dry weather. It is very hardy to cold.

As the common name suggests, this shrub is by nature a resident of wet ground. It often grows in peaty bogs, but plants are occasionally found on dry stony ground. It occurs from the Coromandel Peninsula to Stewart Island, usually at a height of 600 to 1450 metres, although in some South Island areas it is found at much lower altitudes.

Dacrydium biforme
Yellow pine

A large, slow-growing shrub or small tree that seldom reaches a height of more than four or five metres in cultivation. It has distinct juvenile and adult foliage, similar to *D. bidwillii*, but the difference between the two forms is more obvious and even on mature trees there is a tendency for juvenile foliage to develop on the ends of the branchlets. The yellow pine likes a rich, moist soil.

In the wild it is found from Tongariro National Park to Stewart Island, up to a height of 1400 metres.

Dacrydium cupressinum
Rimu, red pine

The rimu is one of the most attractive native trees, particularly during its first 50 or so years of growth, when it forms a handsome pyramidal tree with slender, light green, cord-like, cascading branchlets clothing the tree to ground level. The tiny, prickly leaves are closely set all around the branchlets. Mature rimus will reach a great height, but it takes many years before they assume the proportions of forest giants. Even under ideal conditions (a deep, rich, moist

Dacrydium cupressinum, rimu

Dacrydium cupressinum foliage

soil) in a sheltered garden the rate of growth is rarely more than 20 centimetres a year. This slow growth means that a rimu can be planted in quite a small garden without any need to worry about it becoming embarrassingly large in the near future.

Male and female flowers occur on separate trees. The female flower develops into a tiny cone, which is green at first and changes to orange-red with a black cup. According to Salmon (*The Native Trees of New Zealand*), seed is set in some years only.

The rimu is easily the equal of, and often more attractive than, many exotic conifers widely planted in New Zealand gardens. Its graceful form has made it well known among garden enthusiasts overseas. An American handbook on conifers published a few years ago rated rimu as one of the ten best conifers in the world for gardens. It deserves to be planted far more than it is at present.

Although the rimu prefers a moist, rich soil, it will tolerate quite dry conditions once it is well established. It is hardy to cold but should have some shelter where there are strong winds. It is not suitable for planting near the coast where salt winds are likely.

In its native state, the rimu is still widespread throughout New Zealand, occurring on both main islands and on Stewart Island. It has long been a popular timber tree, although nowadays it is not milled nearly as extensively as in the past. The beautifully grained wood is sought after for furniture making and interior finishing.

Propagation of rimus is usually by seed, but plants can also be raised from semi-hardwood cuttings.

Dacrydium kirkii
Monoao

This is quite a rare tree in the wild, occurring in a few isolated groups in the far north from about Hokianga Harbour to the base of the Coromandel Peninsula and on Great Barrier Island. It is also a rarity in gardens and is still hard to obtain from nurseries. It is a handsome tree of tall, cypress-like form. The narrow and leathery juvenile foliage is most attractive and persists for some years. A good, deep soil is required, and plants should be watered thoroughly during extended dry spells. It is moderately hardy to frosts and is really only suitable for mild climates.

Dacrydium laxifolium
Pigmy pine

This dwarf, prostrate shrub is well suited to growing over a wall, on a bank or in a rock garden. The small, slender branchlets grow close together, forming a thick mat of growth that suppresses weeds. It looks striking tumbling over a big rock and it is a most interesting plant for combining with large-leaved dwarf shrubs such as *Pachystegia*. There are several forms of this delightful plant, some having dark blue-grey foliage while others are brownish green in colour. Female plants bear small red fruits.

The foliage colours of the pigmy pine are more pronounced in a sunny situation, although it will grow quite satisfactorily in light shade. It is very hardy to cold. A reasonably rich soil that does not dry out readily is the ideal. Light soils should be made more suitable by incorporating peat prior to planting. Water thoroughly during periods of drought. Drying out during summer is a common cause of failure with this plant when it is grown in gardens.

The natural distribution of the pigmy pine is from about Tongariro National Park southwards to Stewart Island. Usually it occurs in moist ground, at an altitude of approximately 750 to 1250 metres.

Plants can be propagated by cuttings, layers or seed.

Dacrydium laxifolium, pigmy pine

DENDROBIUM
Orchidaceae

This well-known and widely distributed genus of orchids includes many species with large and brightly coloured flowers. The sole New Zealand species has small white flowers, but despite its subtle colour and the lesser size of its blooms, it is nonetheless a charming plant that deserves to be better known.

Dendrobium cunninghamii

A hardy, epiphytic orchid that usually grows high up on tree branches, although at times it attaches itself to rocks and is also to be found growing on stony ground in well-lit places beneath trees. According to Dorothy Cooper (*A Field Guide to New Zealand Native Orchids*), it often grows beneath beech trees where the conditions are to its liking. It occurs throughout both main islands and on Stewart Island.

D. cunninghamii has the largest flowers of the six epiphytic native orchids; they measure up to 2.5 centimetres across. The flowers are white, usually with a touch of purple in the centre, although some forms are pure white. They are produced in December and January and are dotted over the plants, standing out well against the long and thin, light green, bamboo-like leaves and the pale yellow, wiry stems.

In the garden the native dendrobium can be grown on the trunk of a tree in reasonable light. Plants can be attached directly to the trunk, tied in place with wire or a strip of elastic stocking until the roots cling strongly to the bark. Some sphagnum moss tucked in around the roots encourages strong new growth. During the first year or two regular and thorough watering during summer is beneficial. Plants can also be attached to a rock or a slab of tree fern fibre. Several specimens on fern fibre hang from the roof of my shade house, where they flower freely every year, yet the only attention they receive is an occasional watering in summer. Plants can be obtained from some specialist native plant nurseries that provide a mail-order service.

Dendrobium cunninghamii

DIANELLA
Liliaceae

An interesting, grass-like plant with beautiful blue berries.

Dianella nigra
Turutu, blueberry, inkberry

The foliage of turutu is like that of a bold, firm-leaved grass. The upper leaf surface is dark green and shiny, and the leaf edges are slightly rough. It forms close-growing clumps up to one metre in height. In spring it has pretty, star-shaped, light blue flowers, which are followed in late summer by masses of shiny, dark blue berries on slender, much-branched stems. The berries tend to fall easily and are often taken by birds, but even if they are only present for a short time, they are so attractive as to make the plant well worth growing. A partially shaded location is ideal, and the soil should be deep and moist. Turutu can be used in many different situations: as ground cover beneath trees, to line a shady path, as a contrast to bold foliage, or to plant beside a large rock.

Propagation is by seed or division.

DISPHYMA
Aizoaceae

The one species occurring in New Zealand is a prostrate plant that thrives on sand dunes and rock outcrops beside the sea.

Disphyma australe
Horokaka, native ice-plant

The native ice-plant is an excellent ground cover for beach gardens on pure sand. It can be used to stabilise wind-blown sand and it will also thrive on sun-baked banks and crib walls providing there is excellent drainage and frosts are not heavy. The pink or white daisy-like flowers combine effectively with the dark green fleshy leaves and red stems. New plants can

Disphyma australe, the native ice-plant

be grown with ease from cuttings; do not dig up plants from the sandhills for they play an important role in preventing erosion.

Lucy B. Moore, writing of horokaka in *The Oxford Book of New Zealand Plants*, states: 'On some islands where sea-birds nest on the ground in thousands, this species constitutes most of the vegetation as it is one of the few plants that can tolerate concentrated and continuous quantities of guano.'

DODONAEA
Sapindaceae

The only native species is a tough coastal shrub. The form with purple leaves is most ornamental and is popular with gardeners as an individual specimen and as a hedge.

Dodonaea viscosa
Akeake

Akeake stands up to wind and responds well to clipping, forming a neat, close-growing hedge. The light green, narrow leaves of the species make an interesting contrast with the dark green foliage. It grows reasonably quickly, reaching a height of up to six metres, with a spread of about three metres in an open situation. It can, of course, be kept to a lesser height and width by periodic clipping. Akeake should have a sunny situation. A light to medium soil is preferred and once established, it will survive quite dry conditions. It tolerates moderate frosts; some protection is necessary where frosts are severe.

Akeake is often chosen for windy coastal gardens and exposed hillsides, performing admirably in such situations. Where coastal gales are frequent, some burning of the foliage may occur, and in very windy seaside gardens other natives such as pohutukawa or karo will be more suitable.

Dodonaea viscosa 'Purpurea'
Purple akeake

This handsome form has purple-red foliage, but in other respects it is very similar to the green-leaved species and requires similar conditions. The purple akeake provides colour year round with its striking foliage and deserves to be planted in a prominent place in a shrub border or on a boundary. It looks well in a mixed planting of native shrubs chosen for their interesting foliage and makes a most attractive hedge.

Although the flowers of the native dodonaeas are inconspicuous, the seed-capsules are highly orna-mental and remain on the bushes for some time during the summer. They are useful for floral work. In the case of the green-leaved species, several bushes may be required to produce a good display of seed-capsules, for the flowers are unisexual, with male and female flowers on separate plants. The purple-leaved form, however, seems to be self-fertile and readily produces the seed-capsules even when there is only one bush in the garden.

The wood of akeake is dense and hard and at one time was used by the Maori people for making weapons such as clubs.

Propagation is usually by seed, which germinates freely. The purple-leaved form reproduces true to type. Seedlings are often plentiful beneath established specimens and they will transplant successfully if lifted while small. Winter is the best time for transplanting.

DRACOPHYLLUM
Epacridaceae

There are 32 species of *Dracophyllum* native to New Zealand. They have a distinctive form that makes them extremely interesting for garden use, yet they are little known in cultivation. A few species are prostrate or low growing, but most are shrubs or small trees. Many have grass-like foliage — hence the common name grass tree, which is often applied to the genus as a whole — but some species have broad, recurving foliage in dense clusters, which gives them a dramatic tropical look.

Dracophyllums are slow growing. They require a well-drained soil, but with most species it is important that they should not be allowed to dry out at the roots, especially when becoming established. Soil containing organic matter in the form of peat or leaf mould is ideal.

Propagation is by seed and, in the case of some species, also by cuttings.

Dracophyllum latifolium
Inanga, grass tree

An upright-growing shrub or small tree with slender branches and slim, erect, rigid leaves. The pretty white flowers are produced in slender panicles at the tips of the branches. The common name of grass tree is apt, for it definitely looks like a giant grass. Its highly distinctive form makes it an interesting companion plant for other shrubs and trees with remarkable foliage. It is one of the easier *Dracophyllum* species to grow, being far less fussy about soil type than most. Virtually any soil seems to suit, and once established it is able to withstand reasonably dry conditions.

Plants can be propagated by seed or cuttings.

Dracophyllum strictum
Totorowhiti

A small, much-branched shrub, with attractive, rather short, broad green leaves, which are tinged with red and tapered at the ends. It is usually less than a metre high and is most attractive and highly distinctive. Small white flowers are produced in long and slender

Dracophyllum latifolium

panicles at the tips of the branches. The flower display is most appealing and continues over an extended period, usually starting in spring and continuing until late autumn.

This delightful shrub should be grown in far more gardens. It is well suited to a shrub border or a rock garden, preferring slightly moist soil with plenty of humus. Ideally, it should be shaded from afternoon sun but it will grow in the open.

It can be propagated by cuttings as well as by seed. Plants can usually be obtained from some of the specialist native plant nurseries.

Dracophyllum traversii
Mountain nei nei

This is one of the most striking of all the *Dracophyllum* species. In time it will grow to 10 metres or more and form a stout trunk. Fat tufts of broad foliage provide it with an appearance akin to the cabbage tree but far more unusual and dramatic. The greenish foliage is often spotted with red. A moist, peaty soil and thorough watering during dry weather are needed for this plant to succeed, but even when conditions are to its liking, the rate of growth is very slow.

Occasionally plants can be obtained from a specialist nursery.

DYSOXYLUM
Meliaceae

The sole New Zealand species of the genus *Dysoxylum* is endemic. It is a medium-sized tree with an unusual

Dysoxylum spectabile, kohekohe

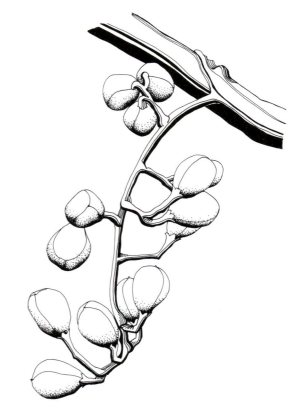

Dysoxylum spectabile berries

flowering habit.

Propagation is by seed, which germinates freely.

Dysoxylum spectabile
Kohekohe

Kohekohe is a handsome tree, easily distinguished by its glossy, green leaves, rounded form and cylindrical trunk. The most striking feature of all, however, is the way in which the flowers are produced. Drooping panicles of waxy white blooms arise from the bare limbs and trunk in early winter. The display is striking but can go unnoticed unless one stands beneath a tree and looks up into the branches. The light green seed-capsules that hang in big bunches are also decorative. They take up to 15 months to ripen, eventually splitting open to reveal the showy, scarlet arils that enclose the seeds.

In gardens the kohekohe seldom exceeds a height of eight metres or so, although old trees in the wild can reach twice this height. It is a fast-growing tree, suitable for background planting or as a specimen where there is room. It is one of those trees that gains in appeal as it ages. Unfortunately, it is not cold hardy and is only suitable for mild districts where the frosts are light. When planted in exposed situations, kohekohe should be provided with some shelter from prevailing winds. A reasonably rich soil is preferred.

It is surprising that kohekohe is so seldom planted, although it must be admitted that its size makes it unsuitable for small gardens and its dense habit of growth can be a disadvantage if it is in the wrong position. Hard cutting back is possible — the new growth comes away quickly — but pruning must be carried out with care if the tree's form is not to be spoilt. It is better to cut the odd limb right back to the trunk rather than leave stumps that will shoot into a mass of new growth. The timber is said to be good for furniture, bearing a resemblance to mahogany, which belongs to the same plant family. Occasionally kohekohe is called New Zealand mahogany.

EARINA
Orchidaceae

There are two species of these epiphytic orchids native to New Zealand. They have attractive and noticeably scented flowers and are suitable for growing in gardens. Plants can be attached to a tree trunk or a slab of fern fibre as described for *Dendrobium cunninghamii*. Both species are cold hardy. Plants can be obtained from some specialist native plant nurseries.

Earina autumnalis
Raupeka, Easter orchid

The flowers of this orchid are noted for their sweet, strong scent, which often becomes obvious before one is close enough to notice the flowers. It is usually an upright grower although it is occasionally drooping. The flowers are a little larger than those of *E. mucronata*, measuring up to 13 millimetres across. They are white with an orange-yellow lip and are produced in clusters at the tips of the stems from February to April.

Earina mucronata
Hanging tree orchid

This is a graceful orchid, with long, slender, weeping stems and narrow leathery leaves up to 7.5 centimetres long. The stems vary in length from 30 centimetres to one metre. The small, dainty, creamy yellow, sweetly scented flowers are produced on drooping sprays at the ends of the stems during October and November.

ELAEOCARPUS
Elaeocarpaceae

Two species of this genus are endemic to New Zealand. They are both tall trees and one, *E. dentatus*, is a worthwhile garden subject.

Elaeocarpus dentatus, hinau

Elaeocarpus dentatus
Hinau

Mature specimens of hinau in the wild are round-headed trees up to 18 metres high. In cultivation it is a slow-growing tree and it would take many years before anything near the ultimate height was attained. During the early stages of growth it has an upright form; the round-headed canopy of foliage develops later. The long, narrow, dark green leaves of hinau are most pleasing and it is a good choice for including in a mixed planting of trees or as a solitary specimen. The pretty white flowers, which occur from November to December, bear a resemblance to lily-of-the-valley. It usually takes some years before trees reach flowering size. The small purplish fruits that follow the flowers are not very conspicuous but they are a popular food for the native pigeon. In pre-European times the Maori gathered the berries in great quantities and, after lengthy preparation, made them into bread or a pudding-like cake.

Hinau should have rich, deep soil that does not dry out. It will grow in sun or partial shade.

Propagation is by seed.

The other native species, *E. hookerianus*, is a slow-growing tree and passes through several juvenile stages of growth before assuming the adult habit. It is generally considered to be of little interest from a horticultural viewpoint.

ENTELEA
Tiliaceae

The genus *Entelea* contains only one species, the handsome and distinctive *E. arborescens*.

Entelea arborescens
Whau

In addition to being one of the fastest-growing native trees, whau is also notable for its big, light green, rounded leaves, which give it a decidedly tropical appearance. Each leaf can be as long as 50 centimetres. The pretty white flowers are produced in abundance during November, and a tree in full bloom is most attractive. The spiky, burr-like seed-pods that follow are also ornamental and they remain on the tree for some time. According to Lucy Moore (*The Oxford Book of New Zealand Plants*), one tree is capable of producing a million seeds in one season.

Despite its rapid growth, whau seldom exceeds a height of seven metres in cultivation. As well as making a most distinctive specimen in the garden or providing a means of rapidly filling a gap, this interesting native can also be grown as a container plant and has possibilities for use as an indoor plant.

Whau is tender, withstanding only very light frosts. It requires a sunny, open situation, shelter from strong

Entelea arborescens seed-pods

winds, and is best in a good, deep soil, although it will grow in light soils. Once established, it is drought tolerant. Unfortunately, it is often short lived but its rapid growth means that it is easily replaced if desired.

Propagation is usually by seed, which germinates readily. It can also be grown from cuttings.

An interesting point about whau is that the wood is extremely light, weighing less than cork when dry. The pre-European Maori used it to make floats for fishing nets. In nature it grows on the Three Kings Islands, around the coast of the upper North Island, and in localised areas as far south as Nelson and Golden Bay.

EPACRIS
Epacridaceae

The two species of *Epacris* that occur in New Zealand are endemic. One in particular, *E. pauciflora*, is a charming garden plant but is little known in cultivation.

Epacris pauciflora
Tamingi

A slender, erect shrub, which grows to a height of 0.75 to one metre in cultivation. It has very small and neat bronze-green foliage, which combines attractively with the compact clusters of shiny, white flowers. This charming plant can be accommodated

in a rock garden or planted with other dwarf shrubs, such as some of the hebes. It blooms most profusely in spring, but often produces some flowers at odd times throughout the year. A well-drained but not dry soil is recommended, and it seems to grow happily in either full sun or light shade. It is hardy to cold.

Plants are propagated by seed.

EUPHORBIA
Euphorbiaceae

The sole New Zealand species is a coastal plant, growing in beach sands and rocks near the water. It occurs on both main islands as well as on Stewart Island and the Chathams. It is also native to Norfolk Island.

Euphorbia glauca

A small herbaceous plant with upright, reddish stems and soft, blue-green leaves. It grows to a height of 30 to 50 centimetres and is of interest as a contrast plant among grasses and small shrubs and for planting among rocks. It has showy, maroon-tipped bracts surrounding the insignificant flowers. Poor, very well-drained soils and hot, sunny situations suit it to perfection, and it thrives near the sea. The sap is thick and milky, a common characteristic of euphorbias.

Euphorbia glauca

FESTUCA
Gramineae

A genus of grasses, one species of which, *F. coxii*, is of interest for gardens.

Festuca coxii

A dwarf grass with slender, silvery blue tufts of weeping foliage. This species is popular for growing in rock gardens or on a low wall, and adds interest when included in a collection of ornamental native grasses, the colouring combining particularly well with the bronze-foliage *Carex* species. It is also an interesting plant to grow among dwarf native shrubs such as some of the hebes, as it provides contrasting form and texture. A sunny situation brings out the best foliage colour, and it should have a well-drained, reasonably rich soil. It is hardy to cold and stands up well to wind but not salt winds.

Plants are easily increased by division.

FUCHSIA
Onagraceae

New Zealand's four native fuchsia species vary considerably in their habits of growth. One, *Fuchsia excorticata*, kotukutuku, a fast-growing small tree, is the largest fuchsia in the world. The other three species include a shrub (*F. colensoi*), a scrambling climber (*F. perscandens*), and a charming prostrate creeper (*F. procumbens*). Of the four species, only two, *F. excorticata* and *F. procumbens*, are reasonably well known as garden plants and readily available from nurseries. The other two can sometimes be obtained from nurseries specialising in native plants.

Festuca coxii

Fuchsia excorticata
Kotukutuku

Kotukutuku is often referred to as the tree fuchsia, and this appropriate common name should be borne in mind when considering where or if to plant it in a garden. A feature of mature trees is the peeling, light brown bark, and they also have an interesting twisted shape, which should not be ruined by pruning in an attempt to maintain a compact form. Tree fuchsias will grow from three to five metres in cultivation, sometimes more, and need room to spread.

The pendulous flowers, produced from early spring to early summer all along the younger branches and sometimes from the older wood as well, are red and purple with purple pollen. They are most attractive but are small enough to go unnoticed at times. Rich in nectar, they attract native birds such as the tui. There are two flower forms seen in the wild — hermaphrodite and female — but it is the brighter hermaphrodite form that is offered for sale by nurseries. Berries follow the flowers, changing in colour from green through red to purple-black when ripe. The ripe berries are juicy and edible, and are sometimes collected for making into jam. The Maori name for the berry is konini, and in some districts, particularly the West Coast, the tree itself is known as konini.

Fuchsia procumbens

Fuchsia excorticata

F. excorticata loses all its leaves where winters are cold, but in districts with a mild climate it is only partly deciduous. It is hardy to cold and grows readily in most soil types but it should not be too dry, especially when first planted out, and should have some shelter from wind. There is a purple-foliage form, *F. excorticata* 'Purpurea', which can be obtained from specialist native plant nurseries.

F. excorticata is found throughout New Zealand and is especially common on the edge of forest areas and where growth is re-establishing after slips or fires. An interesting point about this fuchsia is that it is capable of withstanding fire and will come into new growth again after being subjected to fires that destroy other trees.

Propagation is by cuttings, which strike readily, or by seed.

Fuchsia procumbens

This attractive plant has many uses in the garden, proving interesting on a bank or low wall, for a rock garden — the prostrate habit and thick, pale green foliage are given added emphasis when it is planted beside a bold rock — in the foreground of a shrubbery and as a ground cover. It also makes a novel subject for a hanging basket. It will grow well in most garden soils and is reasonably hardy, although where frosts are heavy it should be grown in a sunny spot in a well-drained soil. Where winters are not severe, it will grow readily in sun or shade. It is inclined to become a little rampant at times, but this habit is easily kept in check by a light trimming in winter when it is bare of leaves.

F. procumbens flowers from about December to February. The pale orange-yellow flowers, tipped with blue pollen, are small but quite remarkable. They are held erect instead of drooping like most other fuchsias and have no petals, and the sepals are reflexed. The flowers are followed by large bright red berries, which are highly ornamental.

F. procumbens occurs in nature in a few coastal sites in the Far North, from North Cape to Coromandel Peninsula. It is becoming increasingly rare in its natural habitat and is regarded as an endangered species. Fortunately its popularity as a garden plant will ensure that it is preserved in cultivation, if not in the wild.

Propagation is by cuttings or layers.

GAULTHERIA
Ericaceae

New Zealand has eight species of *Gaultheria*. All are endemic except for *G. depressa*, which also occurs in Tasmania. They are interesting, cold hardy shrubs, varying in habit from sprawling prostrate growers to bushy shrubs two metres tall. Some species have showy berries; others are outstanding for their flowers. Gaultherias are slow growing and take some

time before they become established and give of their best, therefore patience is called for.

Plants are obtainable from some of the specialist native plant nurseries.

Gaultheria antipoda
Bush snowberry

An upright-growing, small shrub. The white flowers are followed by showy berries, which vary in colour from white to pink and red. An interesting shrub but slow to establish. Plant in a good, moist soil rich in humus.

Propagate from seed.

Gaultheria oppositifolia
Niniwa

One of the larger species, forming a much-branched shrub up to two metres in height. It is distinguished from the other species by its larger leaves. The flowers are white and look like lily-of-the-valley, and a shrub in full flower is a beautiful sight. It likes a lightly shaded situation and is an interesting companion plant for rhododendrons, azaleas and other shrubs that like similar conditions. Plant it in a good, well-drained soil rich in humus and mulch with peat. It is cold hardy.

Gaultheria rupestris
Rock snowberry

A low-growing alpine species that makes an attractive rock garden plant. White bell-shaped flowers are produced in clusters at the ends of the branches, usually in December. A plant that is growing happily will often become covered with blooms, making a most appealing display. It likes a well-drained soil containing plenty of humus. Light soils should have a good quantity of peat incorporated before planting. Full sun or light shade seem equally suitable.

GERANIUM
Geraniaceae

There are five native *Geranium* species, but only two, *G. sessiliflorum* and *G. traversii*, are good garden subjects. The remaining species are too much like weeds for most people's tastes.

Geranium sessiliflorum

This hardy plant occurs throughout New Zealand, growing on scree slopes and stony places from sea level to 1100 metres. The foliage colour varies in different localities from dark green to deep bronze. The small white or pink flowers are produced from mid to late summer. This is an interesting plant for rock gardens although it is not as showy as *G. traversii*.

It should have excellent drainage and an open, sunny situation. A mulch of fine gravel around plants will help to simulate natural conditions.

Plants are easily raised from seed.

Geranium traversii

By far the most attractive of the native geranium species, *G. traversii* is from the Chatham Islands, where it grows on coastal cliffs. This low, spreading plant is delightful in a rock garden or on a raised bed. The leaves are an attractive greyish green and they combine effectively with many small native shrubs and also look well with bronze-leaved grasses. The pink-flowered form is the most popular and the most readily available, but there is also a white-flowered form. Both colours are sometimes available from specialist native plant nurseries.

G. traversii should be grown in a well-drained soil and in full sun. A mulch of stone chips around the base of the plant will keep the roots cool and simulate the plant's natural habitat. Dry conditions will encourage a more compact habit and bring out the best foliage colour.

Plants are easily propagated by seed or by removing rooted offsets.

GNAPHALIUM
Compositae

There are about 12 native species of *Gnaphalium*, but only one, *G. keriense*, is grown in gardens to any extent and it is usually the only one offered for sale by native plant nurseries.

Gnaphalium keriense

This low-growing, spreading native, with its grey-green leaves and heads of white, everlasting daisy flowers on long stems, makes a distinctive garden plant. The flowers are produced in spring and often continue well into summer. In nature *G. keriense* is found on streamsides and damp banks and roadside cuttings, in sun and shade, throughout the North Island and in the upper South Island. In cultivation it is often a more attractive-looking plant than in its wild state. In gardens it should be grown in a sunny situation. Any average garden soil will prove suitable but it should not be allowed to dry out. A few stones placed around the base will benefit the plant by keeping the root system cool.

Plants are easily propagated by cuttings. They can also be raised from seed.

GRISELINIA
Cornaceae

There are two native *Griselinia* species. *G. littoralis* is outstanding as a coastal shrub and *G. lucida* is one of the most handsome of native foliage trees.

Gnaphalium keriense

Griselinia littoralis
Broadleaf

This small, dense-leaved tree is remarkable for its ability to withstand fierce gales and to grow in very poor, dry soils. The dark green, glossy, thick foliage is unaffected by salt-laden winds, and the tree is a popular provider of shelter for gardens near the sea. It will also grow happily in inland gardens and tolerate heavy frosts. It responds well to clipping and is popular as a coastal hedge, although it is not as widely used for this purpose as it deserves to be. With regular pruning it can be kept as a large, rounded shrub. Left to grow in its natural form, it develops into a handsome, round-headed tree, eventually reaching a height of nine metres in a sheltered situation. In very exposed conditions the height is likely to be much less. It combines well with other native trees and shrubs in a mixed boundary planting. Broadleaf is one of those trees that gains in appeal as it ages, developing a gnarled trunk that provides definite character.

The simplest method of propagation is by semi-hardwood cuttings, which strike readily.

Griselinia littoralis 'Taranaki Cream'

This new cultivar has bold, irregular splashes of cream on the leaves. It is a far more colourful plant than *G. littoralis* 'Variegata' and makes a striking subject for a mixed shrub border or grown as a solitary specimen. The foliage colouring stands out superbly against a stained wood fence or house. It is also a worthwhile container plant and is just as hardy as the species.

Propagation is by semi-hardwood cuttings.

Griselinia littoralis 'Variegata'

This variegated-foliage form of broadleaf has an irregular cream margin to the leaves and grey-green and creamy green markings. It is a handsome small tree, every bit as tough and adaptable as the green-leaved form. Usually it does not grow higher than four metres and it can be kept to a lesser height if desired by pruning. Its ability to withstand dry conditions makes it an easily maintained container plant.

Propagate by semi-hardwood cuttings.

Griselinia·littoralis 'Taranaki Cream'·'

Griselinia lucida
Puka

The big, leathery, light green, shiny leaves of *G. lucida* cause it to stand out wherever it is planted. This extremely handsome, small (three to four metres high) tree is ideal as a feature plant for landscaping, yet it is used surprisingly little. The bold foliage provides a tropical effect and makes a pleasing contrast with fine foliage. It can also be grown in a large container. In spite of its lush appearance, *G. lucida* is hardy to cold in most districts and will also stand up well to salt winds and poor sandy soils, making it a useful coastal plant. It will grow with ease in most soil types, in sun or light shade.

In the wild, *G. lucida* often grows as an epiphyte on other trees. It occurs throughout the North and South islands in lowland forests.

Propagation is by semi-hardwood cuttings.

GUNNERA
Holoragaceae

There are approximately eight *Gunnera* species native to New Zealand. They are all small creeping plants. The giant-leaved *G. manicata*, a popular subject for planting beside streams and large ponds, is a native of South America.

Gunnera prorepens

An interesting ground-cover plant for moist soil, forming patches up to 60 centimetres across. It has a creeping habit, rooting down as it goes. The leaves are comparatively large, up to 40 millimetres long by 25 millimetres wide, and are dark brown when the plants are in a sunny situation. In the shade the foliage colour tends to be a brownish green colour. The flowers are rather inconspicuous, but the small raspberry-like berries that ripen about February are most ornamental. *G. prorepens* likes a good soil that does not dry out and should be watered well during periods of dry weather. It makes an attractive contrast plant with stones or rocks beside a stream or natural-style pool.

Plants are easily propagated by rooted runners or by cuttings.

There are several other gunnera species of interest for gardens, but *G. prorepens* is the only one that is readily available and it is one of the most attractive.

HEBE
Scrophulariaceae

Seventy-nine *Hebe* species are native to New Zealand. In addition to the species, there are numerous varieties. Hebes are shrubs that vary in size from prostrate-growing plants ideal for rock or scree gardens to tall, bushy shrubs several metres high. A large number of hebes are of interest for gardens because they have attractive foliage or colourful flowers, and a selection of different hebes will provide flowers year round. Some have flowers over an extended period or intermittently throughout the year.

The 'whipcord' hebes are most distinctive, with tiny scale-like leaves arranged tightly on the branches, making them look like dwarf conifers. Whipcord hebes are better suited to inland gardens with cold winters; they are difficult to grow where the weather tends to be mild and humid. Most hebes are very

Hebe albicans

hardy to cold and wind, are tolerant of dry conditions and will grow in almost any soil providing it is well drained. A few are susceptible to cold, however, notably the large-leaved *H. speciosa* and its hybrids.

Hebes are easily propagated by cuttings.

The following list gives some indication of the great range of hebes which can be grown in gardens. Most of those mentioned should be readily available.

Hebe albicans

This species is outstanding for its foliage, which is a delightful blue-grey colour. It forms a neat, rounded, very compact bush, usually no more than 50 centimetres high. In summer it is covered with white flowers for several weeks. After flowering it pays to nip off the seed-heads to make for a tidier appearance. *H. albicans* is especially attractive when used as a focal point among ground covers or grown in a group of several plants in front of larger shrubs. Cold hardy. Easy to grow. Best in full sun.

Hebe X 'Carnea Variegata' ('Carnea Tricolor')

An attractive foliage shrub that forms a rounded bush a little over a metre high. The narrow leaves are grey-green with an irregular margin of cream. During winter the foliage is flushed with pink. The freely produced flowers are mauve-pink when they open, fading to white as they age. While the flowers are certainly pretty, it is the colourful foliage that is the most striking thing about this shrub. Unfortunately it is only moderately frost hardy.

Hebe chathamica

A prostrate, spreading shrub with rather fleshy, shiny green leaves and spikes of white flowers in mid-summer. It is native to the Chatham Islands, where it is found sprawling over rocks near the sea. A hardy plant for growing in crib walls, on banks or as a ground cover. Likes a well-drained soil. An excellent plant for gardens near the sea.

Hebe cupressoides

This most distinctive and ornamental whipcord hebe has bright green, cypress-like foliage and a symmetrical habit of growth. It grows to a height of one metre. Useful for contrast among other shrubs, providing interesting texture and form. The foliage has a distinctive and not unpleasant aroma. The small purple flowers are attractive but are not always produced freely, which matters little for this shrub is grown primarily for its foliage. This hebe should have a reasonably good, well-drained soil. It is hardy to cold and often grows better in cooler districts. Prune old bushes lightly to keep a compact shape.

Hebe diosmifolia

A compact, bushy shrub up to 1.5 metres high with small, narrow leaves and heads of mauve-blue flowers. It blooms profusely in spring and early summer, and occasionally at other times as well. Attractive for its foliage as well as its pretty flowers. It is usually grown in full sun but will also grow in light shade. Cold hardy. One of the best *Hebe* species for gardens. Several different forms are available, all of which are worthwhile.

Hebe cupressoides

Hebe diosmifolia

Hebe hulkeana

Hebe 'Hartii'

Hebe X *franciscana* 'Blue Gem'

A bushy shrub, up to 1.5 metres high, with attractive green foliage and large violet-blue flowers. An excellent plant for coastal gardens, standing up well to salt winds and dry soils. The main flowering is during mid-summer but it often blooms again in autumn and early winter.

Hebe X *franciscana* 'Waireka'

One of the best variegated-foliage hebes. The broad leaves have a wide margin of creamy yellow around the edges and the colouring is attractive throughout the year. Forms a bushy, spreading shrub up to 60 centimetres high. Makes an interesting ground cover when planted in a group. Stands dry conditions.

Hebe 'Hartii'

An excellent ground cover, this charming prostrate species is one of the most popular hebes with gardeners. It is ideal for planting on a low bank or in a rock garden and is also suitable for planting in a crib wall. Looks delightful among low-growing shrubs or as a cover plant in front of taller shrubs. The small mauve flowers are produced freely, often covering the plant completely in spring. Lesser quantities of flowers occur at other times too. Likes a sunny position. Easy to grow. Cold hardy.

Hebe hulkeana

An unusual and beautiful species. The pale mauve flowers are on long sprays, which develop from the tips of the branches. The flowers, which occur in spring, are dainty and a well-grown plant in full bloom is a spectacular sight. The dark green, shiny foliage is an attractive feature too. This cold-hardy plant is easy to grow providing it has a well-drained, light soil and an open, sunny position. It is not happy in a heavy soil. Excellent for a raised garden that dries out rapidly. Grows readily in sand and is well suited to beach gardens. Cutting off the old flower-heads will keep a compact shape. Avoid hard pruning if possible as this may result in fewer flowers the following season.

Hebe 'Inspiration'

This hybrid hebe is a bushy shrub, usually no more than one metre high. The mature foliage is dark, glossy green and the new leaves are a purplish green. The flowers are purple, fading as they age. It is not an easy colour to live with at times but the free-flowering habit of this shrub makes it worth considering. The main flowering time is early to mid-summer, with a repeat blooming often occurring during late winter. *H.* 'Inspiration' will grow and flower well in sun or shade. Hardy.

Hebe 'La Seduisante'

This hybrid of *H. speciosa* is a handsome, much-branched shrub of 1.5 to two metres in height. It was very popular at one time but is now little known.

It has big purple flowers and large, dark green leaves. The new growths are a purplish green. It is hardier than *H. speciosa* and seems to be untroubled by frosts in most districts. At times the foliage is affected by mildew but this problem is easily controlled by spraying with a fungicide. Flowers profusely in mid-summer and often continues to bloom in odd bursts until well into winter.

Hebe 'Lewisii'

A good hebe for coastal planting as it stands up well to salt winds and dry conditions. Forms a bushy shrub, reaching a height of two metres or more. The slender spikes of attractive flowers are pale violet when they open and fade to white. The main flowering time is winter, with some blooms occurring in summer as well. Needs to mature before the best flowering performances are produced.

Hebe macrantha

A small shrub, usually no more than 60 centimetres high, with pale green foliage. It has a straggly habit of growth and would not warrant a place in most gardens if it were not for the attractive, pure white flowers, which are the largest of any hebe. *H. macrantha* should have a reasonably good, slightly moist soil. It is probably best suited to growing in a rock garden. If plants are trimmed lightly after flowering, a slightly tidier habit of growth should result.

Hebe macrocarpa var. latisepala

An erect shrub, up to two metres high, with large, rather narrow leaves. The flowers are a very dark purple and are produced over a long period, starting in winter and often continuing until late spring or early summer. A most attractive shrub.

Hebe obtusata

A spreading, semi-prostrate shrub that makes a good ground cover or wall plant. It has large leaves and attractive pale lilac flowers over a long period, including winter in mild climates.

Hebe 'Payne's Pink'

This bushy shrub has large green leaves and handsome spikes of bright pink flowers. It is free flowering and makes a great show over a long period. Grows to about one metre. It may need protection where frosts are heavy. There is some confusion about the name of this plant — at times it is listed as *H. speciosa* 'Pink' and 'Pink Payne'.

Hebe pinquifolia

A wide-spreading shrub, rather variable in height. Some forms are little more than 15 centimetres high, others reach to 90 centimetres. The foliage is small and grey-green with a red margin. A most attractive species for a rock garden or the foreground of a shrub border.

Hebe 'Lewisii'

Hebe macrantha

Hebe macrocarpa var. *latisepala*

Hebe 'Payne's Pink'

Hebe speciosa

An outstanding hebe, with large reddish purple flowers that stand out against the broad, dark green, shiny leaves. The flowers are produced over many months. It is a rounded, bushy shrub and will reach a height of one to 1.5 metres. An excellent plant for landscaping, with a pleasing form and interesting foliage as well as bright flowers. Unfortunately it is not completely hardy to cold and may suffer some damage in areas where heavy frosts are experienced. A good shrub for coastal gardens as it stands up well to strong winds and tolerates poor, dry soils.

Hebe speciosa 'Variegata'

The large leaves have grey-green markings and a broad margin of cream. During winter the younger foliage is tinted with pink. It has large reddish purple flowers. This most attractive shrub adds a bright splash of colour in a shrub border. Where heavy frosts occur, it needs a sheltered spot.

Hebe 'Sutherlandii'

A low growing, wide-spreading shrub, which grows to a height of 30 to 40 centimetres. The leaves are small and grey and it has small white flowers. A good plant for a rock garden or for planting in the foreground of a shrub border. With its close growth and spreading habit, it makes an effective weed-suppressing cover plant.

Hebe 'Youngii'

A low-growing, spreading shrub with small, dark green foliage and dark purplish stems. The small purple flowers are produced in summer. This is a pretty little plant for a rock garden or to spill over the edge of a path. Seldom grows higher than 25 centimetres. It is best in a sunny spot. Very hardy to cold.

HEDYCARYA
Monimiaceae

The one species of this genus that occurs in New Zealand is endemic.

Hedycarya arborea
Porakaiwhiri, pigeonwood

An upright tree, five to 10 metres high, with attractive, dark green, shiny, oval to oblong-shaped leaves. The

Hebe speciosa

greenish flowers are inconspicuous but they have a strong and pleasant scent. Male and female flowers are on separate trees. Trees of both sexes must be growing in close proximity before the small but colourful orange-red berries are produced. The berries are a favourite food of the native pigeon, hence the common name.

Pigeonwood is too large to be accommodated in small gardens, but where there is room, it makes a good specimen tree. It requires a good, deep, moist soil and should have shelter from strong winds. During its first few years it is liable to damage by frost and should be protected in colder districts. Once established, it stands frosts well.

Plants can be propagated by seed or cuttings.

HELICHRYSUM
Compositae

The nine New Zealand species of *Helichrysum* are endemic. Seven are small, shrubby plants with cord-like foliage, which are of interest for rock gardens. The two remaining species are creeping plants, one of which *(H. filicaule)* is insignificant, the other *(H. bellidioides)* very showy, with its prolific displays of white everlasting flowers. All the native helichrysums are cold hardy. They require a well-drained soil and are best in full sun.

The easiest method of propagation is by cuttings but they can also be raised from seed.

Helichrysum bellidioides

A prostrate species that is a delightful cover plant beneath shrubs or on a sunny bank. If planted on top of a low wall, it will cascade down for a metre or more and it is also well suited to a rock garden. If planted alongside small shrubs (it combines well with *Hebe hartii*) it often twines through the other plants in a pleasantly natural style. The attractive foliage is grey-green on the upper surface with a covering of matted white hairs on the underside. The flowers are produced in spring and stand above the foliage on slender woolly stems. *H. bellidioides* varies considerably in the wild, some forms having much larger leaves and flowers than others. Plants sold by nurseries are usually selected forms, which are most worthwhile.

This plant is very easy to propagate by rooted runners as well as by cuttings.

Helichrysum coralloides
Coral shrub

A very distinctive plant, which really does look like a piece of coral. Stout branchlets covered with overlapping leaves are arranged tightly against the stem. Between the leaves there is sufficient gap for some of the underlying woolly hairs on the stems to show through, contributing to the unusual appearance. Small yellow flowers are produced on the tips of the branchlets. In cultivation, *H. coralloides* will grow to a height of 30 centimetres.

This is very much a plant for the rock garden enthusiast. In nature it is confined to rock outcrops in the Marlborough mountains, and its very well-drained, rocky habitat should be duplicated to some extent in cultivation. The addition of fine gravel and sand will be of benefit, and if the plant is in a raised position and nestled between rocks, then so much the better. A surface mulch of gravel chips will also be of benefit. An open, sunny situation is necessary.

Helichrysum intermedium (Helichrysum selago)

This small, much-branched shrubby plant, up to 35 centimetres high, is also a most interesting subject for a rock garden. The tiny, dark green leaves are usually outlined by the dense white hairs that cover the stems beneath the tightly packed foliage. It is similar in appearance to some of the whipcord hebes and is sometimes mistaken for one. Plant it in full sun in a free-draining, gritty soil mixture. It is suitable for growing in a stone trough, or in a clay pan or pot, as well as in rock gardens.

Also of interest for the rock garden are *H. plumeum* and *H. parvifolium.*

Helichrysum intermedium

Helichrysum bellidioides

HIBISCUS
Malvaceae

Two species are native to New Zealand. Both are now extremely rare in the wild, being confined to a few frost-free localities in the Far North. They also occur in the tropical islands of the South Pacific. *H. trionum* is often grown as an annual in New Zealand gardens. Neither species has the flamboyant flowers typical of the widely grown hybrid hibiscus.

Hibiscus diversifolius

The lesser known of the two species, *H. diversifolius*, is seen in gardens only occasionally. It is a handsome shrub, 1.5 to two metres high, with small prickles on the stems and leaves divided into several segments. The pale yellow flowers, which have dark purple-brown centres, are large and showy but remain cupped instead of opening wide like those of *H. trionum*. This shrub is easy to grow, providing it has a well-drained soil and a warm, sunny spot. Only light frosts can be tolerated and even these may cause damage, but affected plants will usually produce new growth again the following spring. Hard cutting back each spring will encourage compact growth.

It is easily propagated by cuttings or seed.

Hibiscus trionum

This charming plant is an annual or biennial. It self-sows freely and once established in a garden, will come up each year of its own accord. The pale yellow flowers, with conspicuous purple centres, are produced in great numbers during late spring and early summer. They make a great show, covering the upper stems of the low-growing (up to 60 centimetres) plants. The dark green leaves are narrow, much divided, with serrated edges and covered with silky hairs. *H. trionum* grows easily in a sunny, open situation and a well-drained soil. The habit of growth varies according to the soil type; in light, dry sands plants are often prostrate, while in richer soils they are usually more upright. A reasonably mild climate is the most suitable.

H. trionum is an interesting plant for the front of a shrub border or planted in a drift beside a path. It can look particularly effective when planted among rounded boulders of interesting textures and colours.

Plants are readily raised from seed.

HOHERIA
Malvaceae

The genus *Hoheria* occurs only within New Zealand. The five species are all small to medium-sized trees, which are most attractive in flower. *H. populnea* is the most popular, but the other species are all worthwhile and deserve to be better known than they are at present. The inner bark of these trees has a lace-like pattern, hence the common name lacebark. All species are cold hardy and grow easily in any reasonably good, well-drained soil.

Plants can be propagated by seed or cuttings. The variegated and coloured-foliage cultivars of *H. populnea* are propagated by cuttings only.

Hoheria angustifolia
Narrow-leaved lacebark

This species is distinguished by its small, narrow leaves, which have fine serrations. It undergoes a juvenile stage during which it is a bushy shrub with rounded foliage. When mature, it can grow as high as seven or eight metres. It flowers about January, the small blooms completely covering the tree and making a spectacular show. Makes a striking individual specimen where there is room. It can be kept low by regular pruning.

Hoheria glabrata
Mountain ribbonwood

A spreading deciduous tree up to 10 metres high. Its large, shiny, green leaves turn yellow in autumn before they fall. The pretty, sweetly scented white flowers, produced in mid-summer, closely resemble those of a single cherry. This is a most attractive tree, which, although it will grow in most districts quite satisfactorily, is best in high-rainfall areas. In a dry climate the similar *H. lyallii* is more satisfactory.

Hoheria populnea
Houhere, lacebark

One of the most popular flowering trees among the native flora, *H. populnea* is a fast-growing, erect tree. It usually reaches a height of five to six metres in gardens and is a good choice for planting as a background tree or on a boundary. Its rapid growth rate makes it useful for planting as quick shelter and screening in new gardens. The flowering display of *H. populnea* is most impressive, with beautiful white, pleasantly fragrant blooms being produced in such numbers that the dark green foliage is almost hidden. The flowers occur between February and April, often a time when gardens lack colour. *H. populnea* will grow in quite poor soils but it is at its best in a good, reasonably rich, well-drained soil. There are a number of cultivars of *H. populnea* with coloured or variegated foliage. The following are especially attractive.

Hibiscus trionum

Hoheria populnea

Hoheria populnea 'Alba Variegata', a variegated lacebark

Hoheria populnea 'Alba Variegata'

A magnificent variegated-foliage tree. The dark green leaves have wide and irregular margins of creamy white. Some of the leaves are almost all white; others are mostly green and the new growths often show a touch of pink. It is a bushy tree and makes a gorgeous splash of colour, showing up especially well when seen next to dark green foliage. This tree can be grown in the open or where it receives sun for part of the day only. Where the summers are long and hot, it may pay to choose a site where there is a little shade from afternoon sun. A reasonably rich, well-drained soil will produce the best results from this handsome lacebark.

Hoheria populnea 'Variegata'

The dark green leaves have a large and irregular central blotch of bright yellow. It is a most attractive variegated-foliage tree but it tends to suffer in comparison with *H. populnea* 'Alba Variegata', which is more popular in gardens and is the more striking of the two. *H. populnea* 'Alba Variegata' is also, according to Metcalf (*The Cultivation of New Zealand Trees and Shrubs*), more reliable in areas that experience heavy frosts.

Hoheria sexstylosa
Long-leaved lacebark

Similar to *H. populnea*, but with longer, narrower leaves, which are deeply toothed. The flowers are smaller than those of *H. populnea* but are produced abundantly and are sweetly scented. The branches tend to weep, creating a graceful effect. It makes a handsome specimen tree, well deserving of a prominent position in a garden. Flowering time is February to April.

HYMENANTHERA
Violaceae

A genus of shrubs closely related to *Melicytis*. (Some species of *Hymenanthera* have recently been moved to the genus *Melicytis*.) Most are of interest to collectors of native plants only, for although they are distinctive, they have limited value as ornamentals. However, one or two species, of which *H. chathamica* is probably the most notable, do make attractive garden shrubs.

Hymenanthera chathamica

An upright shrub, usually less than two metres in height, with lance-shaped, pale green, leathery leaves. Small bell-shaped purple and cream flowers are borne profusely along the branches in spring. A bush in full flower is quite ornamental as well as distinctive. *H. chathamica* is hardy to cold and will grow with ease in most soil types. A sunny situation seems the most suitable but it will also grow in shade.

Propagation is by seed or cuttings of firm tip growth.

In nature this species occurs only on the Chatham Islands.

JOVELLANA
Scrophulariaceae

There are two species of *Jovellana* native to New Zealand. One, *J. repens*, is a low, creeping plant of little interest for gardens. The other, *J. sinclairii*, is an attractive but little-known shrub, which does well in cultivation.

Jovellana sinclairii

J. sinclairii is a loose-branching shrub, up to one metre high, with soft, serrated leaves. The attractive pouch-shaped flowers, which are white with purple spots, are produced in mid-summer. This free-flowering plant is best grown in shade, in a humus-rich soil that does not dry out. It should have shelter from wind and heavy frosts.

Plants are propagated from cuttings or seed.

KNIGHTIA
Proteaceae

The sole New Zealand species of *Knightia* is endemic. It is a handsome tall tree suitable for planting as a specimen in a large garden.

Knightia excelsa
Rewarewa, New Zealand honeysuckle

A tall tree, which stands out in any situation on account of its slender, very upright habit of growth and distinctive foliage. The long, narrow leaves are thick and leathery, with serrated edges and pointed ends. The upper leaf surface is dark green, the under surface is much paler and often covered with a thick mat of tiny hairs.

From early spring the unusual reddish bronze flower buds, which have the texture of velvet, can be seen among the leaves, although they are not obvious. In late spring and early summer the red flowers open, and a tree in full flower has a reddish glow about it. It is unfortunate that the flowers are produced well above ground level and are partially obscured by the leaves for they are quite spectacular. An interesting point about rewarewa flowers is that each one is quite small but they are so closely packed in each flower cluster that when they open they look like one large flower. The brown, slightly hairy seed-pods are also quite ornamental but, like the flowers, they have to be seen reasonably close up to be appreciated.

Rewarewa grows to a considerable height (up to 30 metres) in the wild but it is quite suitable for planting in medium- to large-sized gardens. Where a tall, upright specimen tree is required, it is excellent, and when it is seen among trees of contrasting shape, the effect can be most pleasing. This tree is easy to grow in any average, well-drained garden soil, in sun or shade. It will tolerate quite dry conditions but grows

Knightia excelsa seed-pods

Knightia excelsa, rewarewa

slowly when there is a lack of water. It does not stand up well to salt winds.

The natural distribution of rewarewa is throughout the North Island and the Marlborough Sounds. It grows in lowland and lower mountain forests up to an altitude of 850 metres.

Trees can be raised from seed, which ripens in spring.

LEPTOSPERMUM
Myrtaceae

The two species of *Leptospermum* are widespread in New Zealand. *L. scoparium*, the manuka or tea-tree, is to be found in all sorts of situations, from the coast to subalpine regions, and its white flowers are a well-known sight in spring and early summer. Many attractive garden forms with colourful flowers and varying habits of growth have originated from the species, some having been selected in the wild, others resulting from the work of plant hybridists. *L. ericoides*, kanuka, is seldom grown in gardens, which is a pity, for when mature it is an ornamental tree of distinctive form and compares well with many exotics that are planted in great numbers.

Leptospermum ericoides
Kanuka

Usually develops into a small tree but occasionally remains as a large shrub. It can be distinguished from the better-known *L. scoparium* by its smaller and more fragrant white flowers, its softer, darker green foliage and its more tree-like habit of growth. It is worth planting as a specimen tree where it has room to develop clear of other trees, such as in an open paddock or a large lawn. It takes some years before it begins to flower fully and to develop the graceful form typical of mature trees. Manuka blight, a pest that is troublesome with *L. scoparium*, seldom troubles this species. Virtually any well-drained soil is suitable. Cold hardy.

Leptospermum scoparium
Manuka, tea-tree

This species is variable in habit and flower colour. In its typical form it is an attractive large shrub with small, light green leaves and masses of white flowers in spring. It is attractive enough to deserve a place in gardens, and if it were not so common in the wild it would probably be a popular garden shrub. There is no lack of interest, however, in the cultivars with coloured flowers, the best of which are outstanding

A mixed planting of *Leptospermum scoparium* cultivars

Leptospermum scoparium 'Keatleyi'

Leptospermum scoparium 'Tui'

both for their beauty and the abundance of blooms produced. Some of the cultivars flower during winter and a number are of interest for floral work. The cultivars include several that are prostrate growing, which makes them especially suitable for growing on a wall or in a rock garden. The dwarf manukas, labelled the 'nanum' group, have also been bred from forms of *L. scoparium*. They include several gems that are ideal for small gardens.

Manukas are easy to grow, their main requirements being a sunny situation and a reasonably well-drained soil. They are untroubled by cold and wind. Manuka blight is a pest that often causes problems after a few years. It is a sooty mould that grows on honeydew secreted on the bark and foliage by a scale insect. The stems of infected plants become blackened and unsightly, and the plant is weakened. This pest can be controlled by spraying with an insecticide such as Maldison.

The following list of manuka cultivars contains some of the proven favourites. It should be regarded as a guide and not as a definitive list.

Leptospermum scoparium 'Keatleyi'

This is one of the oldest cultivars, having been discovered near North Cape in 1917 by Captain Keatley, a sea captain with a keen interest in the native flora. The very large and abundantly produced single flowers are a beautiful shade of pink. It is still one of the most attractive cultivars and usually flowers over an extended period in spring.

Leptospermum scoparium 'Kiwi'

A delightful small shrub with a compact, close-knit habit of growth, thin branches and tiny leaves. The flowers, which are crimson red, are produced freely in late spring or early summer and last about a month. It is slow growing, with an eventual height of less than one metre. Ideal for small gardens. Combines well with other compact native shrubs such as some of the hebes. A light trimming after flowering will keep the foliage tight and make it an even more attractive plant.

Leptospermum scoparium 'Martinii'

One of the most distinctive manukas. The large flowers are pale pink when they open and change to deep rose as they develop, resulting in two distinct colours of flowers on the shrub at once. The flowers open out over many weeks in late spring and early summer. This most attractive shrub is upright growing, reaching a height of two to three metres.

Leptospermum scoparium 'Red Damask'

One of the brightest manukas, with brilliant crimson flowers produced very freely during late spring and

Leptospermum scoparium 'Red Falls'

Leptospermum scoparium 'Wairere'

early summer. It has dark green foliage tinged with purple and grows in a neat, compact manner. The ultimate height is two to three metres.

Leptospermum scoparium 'Red Falls'

A prostrate manuka with fine bronze-green foliage and dark red flowers, which are produced over a long period commencing in winter and often continuing until late spring. It is an attractive plant to grow on a low wall or in a rock garden where the foliage can cascade or tumble. It is also of interest as a ground cover for the foreground of a shrub border.

Leptospermum scoparium 'Tui'

An erect, small-foliaged manuka with pretty, single, pink, rather small flowers. It is included in the 'nanum' group of manukas, which are usually dwarf, but this one will grow to a height of two metres or more. An attractive shrub, good for combining with shrubs of more rounded form or plants with weeping foliage such as some of the variegated flaxes.

Leptospermum scoparium 'Wairere'

A prostrate shrub with light green, close-set foliage and pretty pink flowers in spring. It has a cascading habit, which is shown off to advantage when it is grown in a rock garden or on top of a wall. It is also an excellent shrub for covering a sunny bank.

LEUCOGENES
Asteraceae

There are two species of *Leucogenes*, both of which are attractive alpine plants suitable for growing in rock gardens. In cultivation they tend to be short lived but are easily propagated by cuttings. They bear a resemblance to the famous edelweiss of the Swiss alps, *Leontopodium alpinum*, hence the common name.

Leucogenes grandiceps
South Island edelweiss

The more difficult of the two species to grow. It must have excellent drainage, a light, preferably gritty, quite poor soil and an open, sunny situation. Wet conditions during winter are likely to prove fatal. Conversely, plants that are kept dry during summer are also likely to die suddenly. Even where conditions are to its liking, this plant tends to be short lived. Fortunately, it is very easy to propagate from cuttings and, ideally, new plants should be kept on hand as replacements.

This very appealing plant grows no more than 10 centimetres in height and has sprawling stems covered with tiny leaves, which are a striking silver colour. The flowers, which occur in summer, are most unusual, each one consisting of flannel-like white bracts surrounding a woolly central flower. In nature this plant grows in crevices or rock ledges in the mountains. In the rock garden similar conditions should be duplicated as far as possible. Tuck the plant in between rocks so that the roots are kept cool. A mulch of stone chips or an underplanting of a tiny prostrate ground cover (the smaller acaenas are good for this purpose) will also help to maintain cool temperatures around the roots.

Leucogenes leontopodium
North Island edelweiss

L. leontopodium is similar to the previous species except that the flowers and leaves are slightly bigger. It is an easier plant to grow, having a greater tolerance of lowland conditions and living longer. It requires

growing conditions similar to those for *L. grandiceps*, except that a slightly better soil is preferred. Both species tend to flower more freely where the winters are cold. Humid conditions, such as those that are common in the Far North, are definitely unsuitable for these plants.

LIBERTIA
Iridaceae

There are four species of *Libertia* native to New Zealand, and all are small plants with white, iris-like flowers. One species, *L. peregrinans*, is widely grown for its stiff, colourful leaves. All are of interest for gardens.

Plants are readily propagated by seed or division of the clumps.

Libertia grandiflora
New Zealand iris

L. grandiflora has large, attractive white flowers, which stand well above the grassy foliage on slender, branched stems. Flowering time is late spring to early summer. This showy plant should have a good soil rich in humus (peat or compost). It does best in light shade, although it will grow in full sun. A good subject

Libertia ixioides

for a mixed flower border or beneath trees, providing the conditions are not too dry.

Libertia ixioides

L. ixioides forms a dense clump of green or yellow-green, tufted foliage. The white flowers are not as showy as those of *L. grandiflora* or *L. pulchella* but it is nonetheless an interesting plant. The brownish orange seed-pods remain on the plants throughout winter. This species will grow in sun or shade, and does well under trees or shrubs.

Libertia peregrinans

L. peregrinans forms clumps of erect, stiff, copper-coloured leaves with prominent orange mid-ribs. It spreads by means of underground runners but is easily controlled by simply lifting unwanted pieces. This is a striking plant, especially when grown in full sun, which brings out the most intense foliage colours. If it is grown through a dense, prostrate ground cover or in association with fine-leaved, cascading native grasses such as some of the *Carex* species, a pleasing contrast in plant forms is created. It is also interesting in combination with gravel or unusual stones and looks dramatic when planted in a large group. *L. peregrinans* also makes a good subject for container growing. I have seen it looking delightful and growing with a minimum of attention in a hollowed-out piece of pumice. A clump thriving in a low container intended for bonzai was similarly effective.

Libertia pulchella

L. pulchella is a dainty, grass-like plant with leaves less than 10 centimetres long and white flowers carried well clear of the foliage on wiry, much-branched stems. The flowers occur in spring and sometimes continue into summer. A lightly shaded situation and a damp, peaty soil are required for this attractive plant.

LIBOCEDRUS
Cupressaceae

There are two New Zealand species. Both are upright, hardy conifers ideally suited for planting as specimen trees, yet they remain little known despite their handsome appearance and the ease with which they grow.

Libocedrus bidwillii
Pahautea, mountain cedar

An upright-growing tree with dense, cord-like, dark green foliage. It has a decidedly narrow habit, which makes it an excellent tree for planting as an individual specimen or for contrasting with rounded plant forms. In the wild it forms a tall tree but it is comparatively

Libocedrus plumosa

slow growing and in gardens takes many years to reach a height of five metres. The very upright habit of growth makes it suitable for quite small gardens.

This very attractive tree is cold hardy and grows well in any average, well-drained garden soil. Thorough watering during dry weather will encourage faster growth. It will tolerate dryish soils but the rate of growth is much slower when grown in such conditions. Full sun or partial shade suit pahautea equally well. It seems to be untroubled by winds, although some shelter should be provided in very exposed sites. It is not suitable for beach gardens; salt winds will cause damage to the foliage.

Libocedrus plumosa
Kawaka

This tree is very similar to *L. bidwillii* in many respects but is distinguished by its more pyramidal shape, finer fern-like foliage and more graceful appearance. It is outstanding and should be planted far more than it is. Its comparatively slow rate of growth may be one reason that it is not grown more, but this is an advantage where there is limited space. Sometimes plants are hard to obtain at general nurseries, but those specialising in native plants (many of which have a mail-order service) usually stock both species. Kawaka requires similar growing conditions to *L. bidwillii*.

Both species can be propagated from seed. Cuttings of semi-hardwood growth can also be taken but this method is not always satisfactory.

Pahautea is found in mountainous forests, usually in high rainfall areas, over much of the country from Mt Te Aroha southwards. Kawaka is less widely distributed, occurring in the North Island from Mangonui southwards to about Rotorua, while in the South Island it is confined to north-west Nelson.

LINUM
Linaceae

A single species of this genus, which includes the true linen flax of commerce, occurs in New Zealand. *L. monogynum* occurs throughout the country, usually on rocky outcrops near the coast.

Linum monogynum
Rauhuia, New Zealand linen flax

A free-flowering, shrubby perennial with wiry stems and pretty blue-green foliage. In cultivation it grows to a height of 60 centimetres and is useful for rock gardens, for growing between paving slabs, on sunny banks and in the foreground of a shrub border. It also looks striking growing in a group among small rounded boulders chosen for their interesting forms and colours. The graceful nature of linum makes it an interesting subject to contrast with bold-foliaged plants such as flax, astelia or pachystegia. It also makes a striking combination with the non-native herbaceous perennial *Hosta sieboldiana*, which has big, corrugated, glaucous leaves.

L. monogynum is drought resistant and extremely easy to grow, providing it has a sunny spot and reasonably well-drained soil. An adaptable plant, it will grow equally well in sandy beach gardens or far inland. It is frost hardy. The pure white, open flowers, produced on the tips of the slender branches, sparkle in the sun and sway with the breeze. The flowering period is lengthy, from early spring until well into summer. After flowering, a light pruning to remove the seed-capsules is recommended to keep the bushes compact and vigorous.

L. monogynum tends to be short lived but is easily and quickly established again from seed. Self-sown seedlings will spring up around mature bushes if a few seed-pods are allowed to remain after flowering.

Linum monogynum

LOPHOMYRTUS
Myrtaceae

Lophomyrtus species are elegant shrubs and small trees with many uses in the garden. There are two species, *L. bullata*, ramarama, and *L. obcordata*, rohutu, as well as a number of cultivars, developed from hybrids between the two species, which are exceptional for their coloured or variegated foliage.

Lophomyrtus bullata
Ramarama

Ramarama is an upright-growing shrub or small tree, which seldom exceeds four metres in cultivation. It is easily distinguished by its small, thick leaves, which are shiny and have an attractive blistered appearance. In shade the leaves are bright green but in the open the foliage takes on bronze-red tints, which are most appealing. The small white flowers occur in summer, and when a tree flowers profusely (something it is more inclined to do when grown in an open situation), the display is attractive. Small berries follow the flowers, turning dark red when they ripen in winter.

Ramarama is an attractive shrub for a mixed planting, its distinctive foliage combining well with other leaf textures and colours. It grows best in a moderately rich soil that does not dry out for long periods. Where the conditions are dry, ramarama is often troubled by thrips, which causes the leaves to turn a silvery colour. Once established, it is hardy to cold in most districts, but where frosts are heavy young plants should be protected at first. It is not suitable for exposed coastal gardens.

Lophomyrtus obcordata
Rohutu

Also an erect-growing shrub or small tree, but with much smaller leaves than ramarama. This slender tree has a graceful appearance when mature and makes an interesting specimen. Its eventual height is usually no more than four metres, making it a useful subject for small gardens. If preferred, it can be kept lower by pruning. Rohutu is also suitable for hedging as it responds well to regular clipping. The small, creamy white flowers and the berries that follow attract native birds.

Rohutu requires similar growing conditions to ramarama although it is hardier to cold. Its natural distribution is in forests throughout the North and South Islands, from sea level to about 1050 metres.

Propagation of both species is by either semi-hardwood cuttings, generally considered the most satisfactory method, or from seed.

Wherever the two species occur together, they hybridise freely. The natural hybrids that occur, known as *L. X ralphii*, are most attractive and the best of these have been selected by nurseries and given cultivar names. The cultivars are among the most popular native trees and shrubs for home gardens. The foliage is also widely used for floral work.

These shrubs are superb for gardens, their slender habit allowing them to be combined easily with many other shrubs and trees, both native and exotic. Their upright nature contrasts well with rounded plant forms. The red-foliaged cultivars such as *L.* 'Kathryn', which has superb, deep reddish brown leaves, are best in full sun. Those with variegated foliage are often better in light shade, particularly *L.* 'Gloriosa', which has small leaves with cream and light green markings and a hint of pink. *L.* 'Gloriosa' is superb for combining with dark green foliage and can be striking when planted in a group in a woodland setting. In my own garden about 10 plants of this cultivar grow in an informal group beside a path, thriving in the woodland conditions created by assorted, long-established taller trees, among them kowhai, pohutukawa and karaka.

Also of interest are the dwarf cultivars. One of the most notable of these is *L.* 'Pixie', which has tiny, bronze foliage and is marvellous for a rock garden, for contrast among ground covers such as *Pimelea prostrata*, or with other small shrubs such as the dwarf hebes.

The *Lophomyrtus* cultivars have similar requirements to the species — a reasonably rich, not too dry soil. They respond well to trimming and some, such as *L.* 'Kathryn', make attractive hedges where the conditions are reasonably sheltered. Most of the cultivars are quite hardy to cold but are not suitable for planting in exposed coastal gardens.

The cultivars can be propagated by cuttings.

Lophomyrtus obcordata berries

Lophomyrtus 'Kathryn'

Some of the best-known lophomyrtus cultivars are:

L. 'Gloriosa'. Small leaves with attractive cream and green markings and a hint of pink. The eventual height is seldom more than two metres.

L. 'Kathryn'. Dark bronze-red foliage, upright habit of growth. Requires full sun to develop the best foliage colours. Popular for floral work. Grows to a height of two to three metres.

L. 'Lilliput'. Dwarf, very attractive dark bronze-red foliage. Popular for small gardens. Leaves are larger than *L.* 'Pixie'.

L. 'Pixie'. Delighful dwarf, very small bronze-green foliage, slow growing.

L. 'Redshine'. Dark green foliage suffused with coppery red. Grows to a height of two metres.

L. 'Traversii'. Green, cream and red foliage. Good for contrast, upright habit, eventually reaches a height of about two metres.

MACROPIPER
Piperaceae

Only one species of the genus *Macropiper* occurs in New Zealand. It is a rapid-growing small tree, generally dismissed as a garden plant, yet it is useful for growing in difficult situations such as deep shade. The variety *majus* has bolder foliage and deserves to be better known than it is at present.

Macropiper excelsum

Macropiper excelsum
Kawakawa

A fast-growing shrub with heart-shaped, smooth and shiny, green leaves. Each leaf is distinctively veined and often the leaves are full of holes of varying size, caused by a chewing insect. The dark brown, shiny stems and lighter bark of the main trunk are also notable characteristics, as are the narrow spikes of flowers, which are present for much of the year. Male and female flowers occur on different plants. The fruits, which are found on the female plants, are packed closely together on the spikes and turn orange when ripe. These fruits provide food for native birds.

Kawakawa grows most readily in a rich, moist soil. However, it will also grow in dry conditions and is useful for those difficult shaded situations such as beneath large trees, where it is often hard to establish shrubs to provide privacy or shelter from ground draughts. Although kawakawa will grow in sun or shade, the latter suits it best. In full sun the leaves usually turn light yellow and look rather unattractive. It is frost tender but if sheltered by overhead trees, it will be unharmed even where frosts are quite heavy. In the garden it self-sows freely. For this reason it is sometimes regarded as a weed, but it can be a most useful and attractive shrub in the right place.

For the Maori of yesteryear, kawakawa was invaluable for its medicinal properties. Its various parts provided cures for or alleviated ailments as diverse as boils and bladder complaints. The early European settlers learnt from the Maori that the scalded leaves of kawakawa encouraged the rapid healing of wounds. The Maori also used the leaves as a means of deterring insects. According to Christina Macdonald (*Medicines of the Maori*), green branches of kawakawa were laid between the kumara beds and burnt slowly. The acrid smoke thus produced kept harmful insects away from the crops. Macdonald also says that early travellers burnt the green branches on their campfires to repel mosquitoes and sandflies.

Kawakawa is easily propagated by seed or cuttings.

It is widespread in the coastal forests of the North Island and the upper half of the South Island and the Chatham Islands.

Macropiper excelsum 'Variegatum'

This variegated form of kawakawa has a patch of yellow in the centre of the leaf. It is an interesting plant but not particularly showy and suffers in comparison with many other native shrubs with variegated foliage, some of which are quite outstanding. It is also inclined to revert to plain green.

This plant can only be propagated by vegetative means (usually cuttings).

Macropiper excelsum var. *majus*

M. excelsum var. *majus* (now renamed var. *psittacorum*) is a striking plant, easily distinguished from the species by its leaves, which are larger, glossier and a paler green colour. It is good for foliage contrast, particularly with smaller-leaved plants, and makes an interesting subject for containers. When grown as a container plant it should be kept well fertilised. I have seen it used most effectively as a feature plant beside a south-facing front door, where the conditions were rather dry because of the overhanging roof.

This variety has a limited distribution in the wild, being found only on some offshore islands including the Three Kings, Poor Knights and Little Barrier.

MAZUS
Scrophulariaceae

There are two *Mazus* species in New Zealand, both small, creeping, perennial herbs. *M. radicans* is of the most interest for gardens. Both species of *Mazus* are cold hardy.

They are easily propagated by lifting rooted pieces.

Mazus pumilo

M. pumilo has lots of small, white or pale blue flowers in early summer. It grows rapidly in moist soil, rooting down as it goes, and is a good cover plant for shade. Where the conditions are to its liking, it may become invasive but is easily removed from where it is not wanted with a little digging.

Mazus radicans

M. radicans, the swamp musk, also roots down as it spreads and will form quite a large mat under good conditions. It should be planted in good soil that does not dry out. Plants grown in full sun flower most freely. The exquisite flowers, which are 1.5 to two centimetres across, are white and purple with a yellow throat. The attractive leaves are mottled and slightly hairy. A highly recommended plant.

Mazus radicans

MELICOPE
Rutaceae

Two species are native to New Zealand but only one, *M. ternata*, is of interest to gardeners. It is widespread among coastal and low-country forests throughout the North Island and the north of the South Island.

Melicope ternata

Melicope ternata
Wharangi

This is a beautiful foliage shrub for the garden yet it is seldom seen in cultivation. It forms a large rounded shrub up to four metres high when grown in the open. Among dense trees it will be drawn up to a greater height. Wharangi has very distinctive, pale green, shiny foliage with a slightly wavy margin. The leaves are aromatic when crushed. The small yellow flowers blend with the foliage and are easily overlooked, but this does not matter for the foliage alone makes this shrub worth growing.

Wharangi is an interesting choice for a mixed shrub border, combining well with other natives as well as with exotics. A deep soil rich in humus is ideal, and it should have some shelter from strong winds and protection from heavy frosts. Under good conditions wharangi grows quickly.

Propagation is usually by seed, which germinates readily, but it can also be grown from cuttings.

MELICYTUS
Violaceae

There are four species of *Melicytus* native to New Zealand and three of these are of interest for garden use although they are seldom seen in cultivation. The best-known species is *M. ramiflorus*, the mahoe or whitewood. *Melicytus* species bear small, brightly coloured berries, which are ornamental and provide food for native birds.

Melicytus ramiflorus, whiteywood

Propagation is by seed, which germinates freely. Small self-sown seedlings, which are usually plentiful near established trees (providing both sexes are present), can be transplanted in winter.

Melicytus lanceolatus
Mahoe wao

A spreading, rounded tree up to four metres high, with narrow, willow-like leaves, which are bright green and toothed on the margins. It forms an attractive specimen tree, which grows easily in any moderately rich garden soil and is hardy to cold. It has prolific crops of berries, although they are not as brightly coloured as those of *M. ramiflorus*.

Melicytus macrophyllus
Large-leaved whiteywood

This tree is similar to *M. ramiflorus* in many respects but is easily distinguished by its larger, more rounded and rather leathery leaves. The berries are white, turning light purple when ripe. The large-leaved whiteywood, with its handsome foliage, makes an interesting specimen shrub or small tree.

Melicytus ramiflorus
Mahoe, whiteywood

A fast-growing small tree with dark, dull green, tapering leaves and a pale creamy grey trunk. It forms a rounded head of dense growth and makes quite an attractive specimen tree. It is also useful for shelter and as an easily established, quick filler. Mahoe responds well to clipping by rapidly making new growth again, and it could be used for hedging. Grows in any reasonable garden soil. Cold hardy.

Mahoe has showy, violet-blue berries, which are quite small but are produced in such quantity that they make a bright display when they ripen in late summer. They are a favourite food of the wood pigeon. Male and female flowers are produced on separate trees, therefore both sexes must be present before berries can occur. The foliage of mahoe is palatable to cattle and in times gone by it was often used to supplement fodder during a drought. At one time the wood of mahoe was used for making charcoal.

MERYTA
Araliaceae

One species of *Meryta* occurs in New Zealand, its natural distribution confined to the Three Kings and Hen and Chickens groups of islands.

Meryta sinclairii
Puka, pukanui

A small, rounded tree, which stands out in any setting on account of its huge, dark green, prominently veined leaves. Puka is undoubtedly one of the most beautiful native trees, noted for its handsome form as well as for the glossy upper surface of the foliage. The undersides of the leaves are pale green.

Puka is easy to grow in any reasonably rich, well-drained soil. It is frost tender, especially when young,

Meryta sinclairii, puka or pukanui

Meryta sinclairii 'Moonlight'

but mature trees will tolerate light frosts although their leaves may show some signs of damage after a cold spell. It is quite happy in light shade, and where frosts are a little too heavy for it to be grown in the open, it is sometimes seen thriving beneath a protective canopy of tall, light-foliaged trees. This versatile tree can also be grown in a large container; a big specimen in a half wine barrel makes a striking feature for a patio or courtyard. In areas where frosts are likely, container-grown specimens can be positioned where they will have overhead protection. Puka also has potential as an indoor plant.

This tree grows surprisingly well in coastal gardens, the foliage proving reasonably tolerant of salt winds. However, the foliage is likely to be larger and lusher when puka is grown in more sheltered conditions and in better soils than those typical of beach gardens.

One of the most appealing features of puka is the tropical mood its bold foliage can give to gardens. It fits in well in virtually any situation, whether grown as a solitary specimen, in a group, among other native trees and shrubs, or even as a street tree in mild districts. Combined with other bold-foliage natives such as *Pisonia brunoniana* 'Variegata', the effect is striking. Other possibilities include using it with colourful cascading flaxes or sprawling variegated-foliage coprosmas, or as a bold contrast to fine-leaved shrubs or trees such as *Lophomyrtus* species.

Puka does have one drawback, which should be remembered when choosing a position for it in the garden. The old leaves tend to fall regularly throughout the year and can be a nuisance in some situations. However, this is a minor fault in such a superb tree.

The large heads of green flowers are of interest and the bunches of berries that follow are very ornamental. The berries are green at first, turning shiny black when ripe, and are a source of food for the native pigeon. Male and female flowers are usually on separate trees, but bisexual flowers occur occasionally.

A variegated-foliage form of puka, *Meryta sinclairii* 'Moonlight', has bold yellow markings on the leaves. It is a beautiful plant but is not nearly as vigorous as the plain, green-leaved species and must have a sheltered position and good soil to succeed. I have seen it growing well in light shade and in a situation where it is kept watered during dry weather.

M. sinclairii is easily raised from seed, which should be fresh. *M. sinclairii* 'Moonlight' is propagated by cuttings.

METROSIDEROS
Myrtaceae

There are 11 species of *Metrosideros* native to New Zealand. Five are trees, the remainder are climbing plants. Included in the genus is one of the most spectacular flowering native trees, *M. excelsa*, pohutukawa, and the brightest flowered climber, *M. carminea*, akakura.

Metrosideros albiflora
Akatea, white rata

Akatea is a woody climber that occurs in the kauri forests. It is seldom seen in gardens, which is somewhat surprising considering its large heads of attractive white flowers. Plants are sometimes hard to obtain, but several native plant nurseries include it in their mail-order lists. Apart from its flowers, this species is also easily distinguished by its broad, leathery leaves. The base of the vine should be in a cool, shaded spot, and a well-drained, moderately rich soil containing peat or leaf mould will give good results. Thorough watering during dry weather is recommended. Akatea seems to be moderately cold hardy.

Propagate by seed, layers or semi-hardwood cuttings.

Metrosideros carminea
Akakura

This spectacular climber has brilliant carmine-red

flowers, produced so abundantly in spring that the dark green foliage is often completely obscured. The stems have small aerial roots, which will cling to any textured surface that provides some grip. It is often seen covering a wall, growing up a lamp post or on a fence. A plant in full flower is an eye-stopping sight. Native birds such as the tui are attracted by the nectar-rich blooms, increasing the pleasure provided by this climber. Akakura should have a cool, moderately rich, well-drained but not dry soil. Ideally, it should be grown like clematis — with the roots in cool shade but the vine able to reach into the sun to flower. A sheltered situation is required. Anything more than light frosts are likely to damage the flower buds that form in autumn.

A curious thing about akakura is that it can also be grown as a shrub. If plants are propagated from cuttings taken from the mature bushy growth that has borne flowers previously, then non-climbing, bushy shrubs will be produced. Both types are usually sold by nurseries. The shrub form makes a stunning combination with *Sophora tetraptera* 'Gnome', the dwarf kowhai, which has large, golden yellow flowers at the same time of year.

Metrosideros excelsa
Pohutukawa

M. excelsa, pohutukawa, is an outstanding tree, which grows with ease in widely varying conditions. It is,

however, by nature a tree of the coast and is hardy only to moderate frosts. Young trees are particularly susceptible to cold and where frosts are anything more than slight, they should be protected during their first few winters. As a coastal tree, pohutukawa is in a class of its own, able to stand up to fierce salt-laden winds in a manner that few other trees, native or exotic, can match. It is drought resistant and will grow in the poorest of soils yet it is also at home in sheltered gardens with rich soils. Its main requirements are good drainage and a sunny site.

Pohutukawa is a handsome, long-lived, rounded tree with dark green, glossy foliage and an open habit of growth. The form of old trees is very pleasing. The summer displays of red flowers are well known to most New Zealanders, as pohutukawas have been planted in many coastal districts over the years.

Although their natural distribution is confined to the upper North Island, they have become a feature of coastal districts much further afield, including milder areas of the South Island such as Nelson, Westland, Banks Peninsula and as far south as Dunedin in some sheltered areas.

Pohutukawa responds well to pruning; even old trees can be cut back ruthlessly and they will soon shoot into new growth. Heavy pruning should only be done where trees have become too large; where possible they should be allowed to develop their natural form. Pohutukawa is excellent as a rugged, durable hedge for coastal districts, but when trimmed

Metrosideros carminea, shrub form

Metrosideros carminea, climbing form

Metrosideros excelsa

regularly, it is likely to have a sparse display of flowers. It can also be used as a container plant, although the Kermadec pohutukawa, in its variegated or plain-leaved forms, is probably a better choice for this purpose.

Pohutukawa is easily raised from seed or cuttings. Self-sown seedlings are often found near established trees and these transplant readily during winter. Even large pohutukawas can be shifted during the winter months. Plants grown from cuttings are likely to start flowering at an earlier stage than seedlings.

Named pohutukawa cultivars that have been selected for their superior flower displays are becoming available and these are most worthwhile.

Metrosideros excelsa 'Aurea'
Yellow pohutukawa

This tree is identical to *M. excelsa* except for the flowers, which are yellow instead of the usual crimson. Although it is not as striking a tree as the typical form, it is still of interest, and if the red and yellow are planted side by side the combination is quite startling.

Metrosideros fulgens
Aka

A robust climber, which has bright orange flowers during late summer and autumn. It can be grown in the same manner as *M. carminea*, as a climber or shrub, and requires similar conditions. It is hardy to cold in most lowland areas.

Metrosideros kermadecensis
Kermadec pohutukawa

The Kermadec pohutukawa comes from the Kermadec Islands, which are 1250 kilometres north-west of the Bay of Islands. It is similar to *M. excelsa* in many respects but the flowers and leaves are smaller. In addition, the foliage is a darker green and more rounded. The flowers are usually produced off and on throughout the year and there are never a great number of flowers at one time. It is smaller than *M. excelsa* — in cultivation the eventual height is seldom more than six or seven metres — which makes it better suited to small sections and as a street tree. The Kermadec pohutukawa is thought to be slightly more frost tender than *M. excelsa*.

Culture and propagation are the same as for *M. excelsa*.

Metrosideros kermadecensis 'Sunninghill'

This less well-known variegated Kermadec pohutu-kawa has a patch of yellow in the centre of the leaf. It is attractive but is not as showy as *M. kermadecensis* 'Variegata' and is more inclined to revert to plain green foliage.

Metrosideros kermadecensis 'Variegata'

M. kermadecensis 'Variegata' has a broad cream margin to its green leaves. This striking plant has become very popular in recent years and is widely used in coastal gardens. It looks very effective when seen against a background of dark green foliage or growing alongside bold-foliaged trees and shrubs such as *Meryta sinclairii*, *Griselinia lucida* or *Pseudopanax arboreus*. It also looks attractive when planted at intervals along a driveway or on a boundary, and can be clipped to form a dense hedge. As a street tree it is superb, for it is not too robust, is long lived and reliable, and requires very little if any attention. *M. kermadecensis* 'Variegata' is also well suited to growing in containers.

Propagation of this cultivar is by cuttings. Seedlings will have plain green foliage.

Metrosideros robusta
Rata

This giant of the native forests is famous for its habit of growth. Usually it starts life as an epiphyte, growing high up in a mature tree. As it develops, roots are sent down to the ground and in time the vine becomes so powerful that it completely envelops the host, which dies, and the rata continues to grow as a tree.

Metrosideros excelsa 'Aurea'

The rata does not have to grow as an epiphyte, however; it is also able to develop without the assistance of a host. In cultivation it forms a tall tree, with dark green, dense foliage. Usually many years go by before the first flowers are seen, and the flower display is not as spectacular as some other species. It is easy to grow in a reasonably rich, well-drained garden soil and it withstands quite heavy frosts.

Metrosideros umbellata
Southern rata

The southern rata is a slow-growing bushy shrub or small tree, with dark green, shiny, pointed leaves. It is often many years before flowering starts, but this should be speeded up if cuttings are taken from growth that has already produced flowers. The deep red flowers are spectacular, occurring in mid to late summer. *M. umbellata* is inclined to flower erratically, producing an abundance of blooms one year and a sparse display the next. It is hardy to cold and grows easily in most soil types providing there is good drainage.

Metrosideros kermadecensis 'Variegata'

MIMULUS
Scrophulariaceae

One species of *Mimulus* occurs in New Zealand. It is seldom seen in cultivation and is rarely offered by nurseries, but its charms are such that it is worth the effort of collecting cuttings, which are easy to strike, from plants in the wild.

Mimulus repens

A small, creeping plant with tiny, dark green, fleshy leaves. It grows in damp hollows in sand dunes and on mud flats in coastal areas. The delicately coloured flowers, which vary from very pale to bright pink and often have a yellow throat, are large in comparison to the foliage, and when plants are in full flower in spring the display is most attractive.

To succeed in gardens, *M. repens* must have a damp, sunny situation — peaty soil is ideal. It is only moderately frost hardy. Slugs and snails are attracted to the foliage and can cause considerable damage, so slug bait should be applied near plants at frequent intervals. *M. repens* tends to be short lived in cultivation, therefore it pays to have replacement plants coming on from cuttings.

MYOPORUM
Myoporaceae

Two species are native to New Zealand; one is a shrub or small tree, the other a ground-cover shrub. Both species are of interest for gardens.

Myoporum debile
Prostrate ngaio

A useful plant for ground cover and for walls and banks. It has narrow, light green leaves and a wide-spreading habit of growth. In autumn small cream flowers are produced and these are followed by berries, which are white with a purplish flush. The berries, which are most attractive, often remain throughout winter.

The prostrate ngaio should be grown in a well-drained soil that is not too heavy. A sunny situation is preferred. It is moderately frost hardy.

Propagation is usually by cuttings, but it can also be raised from seed.

Myoporum laetum
Ngaio

Ngaio is by nature a tree of the coast and stands up well to salt winds, poor sandy soils and dry conditions. A good shelter tree, reaching a height of five to six metres in cultivation, it can also be used as a hedge, although the faster-growing and bushier Tasmanian ngaio, *M. insulare*, has largely displaced it for this purpose.

Ngaio trees are easily recognised by their rounded heads of fresh-looking, bright green foliage and sturdy, spreading branches, their corky, wrinkled bark and the gnarled look that gives mature trees such character. The lance-shaped leaves are rather fleshy and are covered with oil glands, which show up as small spots.

Small white flowers spotted with purple are produced in clusters in the axils of the leaves in summer. These are followed in late summer to early autumn by small, reddish purple fruits.

Ngaio is suitable for use as a specimen in inland gardens as well as near the coast. It is frost tender when young, but once established, it is generally untroubled by moderate frosts. Although ngaio will tolerate very poor soil, it will grow far better in reasonably rich soil. This tree definitely improves with age, and old specimens should be preserved wherever possible. Far too often they are destroyed needlessly without recognition of how much character they can provide for a garden or paddock.

All parts of ngaio are poisonous and must not be eaten. Some parts of the tree were very useful to the Maori — for example, the leaves were rubbed on the skin to repel sandflies. Pioneer farmers are said to have made a sheep dip from a decoction of the leaves when nothing else was available and, according to Macdonald (*Medicines of the Maori*), early veterinarians sometimes used a pack of bruised and warmed ngaio leaves for horses' legs.

In the wild ngaio occurs near the coast, often among other vegetation, although where conditions are particularly exposed it may be the sole species. It is common throughout the North Island and northern South Island, but from Banks Peninsula to Otago, its southernmost limit, it is found only infrequently.

Myoporum laetum, ngaio

MYOSOTIDIUM
Boraginaceae

The genus *Myosotidium* contains one species only, the remarkable *M. hortensia* from the Chatham Islands, considered an aristocrat of the plant world by gardeners in New Zealand and overseas.

Myosotidium hortensia
Chatham Island forget-me-not

This dramatic plant is outstanding both for its foliage and flowers. The big, broad, deep green leaves are shiny and prominently grooved. On a well-grown plant they can be 30 centimetres long and 25 centimetres across at the widest point. In late spring large heads of sky-blue flowers open from paler coloured buds, creating a spectacular display. Occasionally the flowers have a pinkish tinge, and there is also a rare white-flowered form, which comes true from seed.

In nature *M. hortensia* is found only on the Chatham Islands. On the main island it is now rare in the wild, with only a few isolated colonies remaining where plants are beyond the reach of sheep and cattle, which relish the succulent foliage. In former times this magnificent plant grew in a broad band around much of the island, just above the high-tide mark. On some of the smaller uninhabited islands of the Chatham group large numbers of plants still grow in this manner.

That this species will naturally grow happily in exposed situations so close to the sea often puzzles gardeners on the New Zealand mainland, who find

Myosotidium hortensia, Chatham Island forget-me-not

that shaded conditions and a moisture-retentive soil rich in humus are essential for success. These requirements for plants in cultivation are easier to understand when the climate of the Chatham Islands is taken into account. The weather of these isolated islands is mild all year round and there are many cloudy, misty days. Perhaps the most significant point is that where the forget-me-nots grow there usually seems to be a layer of moisture-retentive, peaty soil not far below the surface, even if at first glance the plants appear to be sustained by nothing more than sand and shingle with a surface mulch of paua shell.

Plants should be watered thoroughly during dry weather. It is an ideal subject for massed plantings, as its evergreen foliage is always of interest and provides a bold, sculptural note useful in landscaping.

Propagation is by seed, which sets freely and germinates readily, providing it is fresh. Self-sown seedlings often occur around established plants; these transplant easily during the cooler months of the year if they are lifted carefully.

MYOSOTIS
Boraginaceae

New Zealand has some 35 native species of *Myosotis*, a fact that is surprising considering there are only 50 or so in total. Many of the native species are remarkable for the colour of their flowers — some are yellow or brown, others dark red or almost black. The native species are a challenge to grow — it seems that the most striking species are the most difficult in cultivation — and are best suited to rock gardens. Sharp drainage and a gritty soil are usually vital to success, and damp conditions in winter should be

Myosotidium hortensia in its natural environment on the Chatham Islands

guarded against, particularly with the alpine species. Although a short life in cultivation is to be expected of many of the native *Myosotis* species, they are easily propagated and new plants can be raised to take the place of parent plants. Some species are usually available from alpine plant nurseries and nurseries specialising in native plants.

Myosotis colensoi
Colenso's forget-me-not

Forms a spreading, dense mat of greyish green foliage. During spring it has pretty white flowers. This plant should have a gritty, rather poor soil; in a rich soil it develops a straggly habit of growth. Plant in full sun. Occurs in nature in the Upper Waimakariri Valley, where it grows on limestone rocks.

Myosotis petiolata var. *pansa*

A robust plant with green foliage and small, freely produced white flowers. It seems to be one of the easier species to cultivate and often self-sows freely.

In nature it occurs on the coast north of the Manukau Heads in North Auckland.

MYRSINE
Myrsinaceae

There are nine species of *Myrsine* native to New Zealand. They vary in size from shrubs to small trees, all with interesting foliage and form. The three listed are all small trees that can be used to provide a distinctive character in gardens. They are easy to grow in most situations and soil types.

Myrsine Australis
Mapau

This hardy, small tree occurs throughout New Zealand. It has pretty, light green, wavy-edged foliage, which contrasts with the reddish-coloured bark on the young branches. The old branches have grey bark. Mapau is an excellent foliage plant and is an attractive subject for a mixed planting of shrubs. The fact that it responds well to clipping and pruning means that it can be kept to a desired height or shape and can also be grown as a hedge. It is fast growing and hardy to cold and wind.

Myrsine divaricata
Weeping matipo

A most unusual tree, up to four metres high, with small leaves and stiff, criss-crossed, drooping branches. The small flowers are obscured by the foliage, and the fruits that appear on female trees usually go unnoticed too, but this is of little concern as the tree is grown primarily for its striking form.

It is useful for providing a contrast with other trees and shrubs or as a highly distinctive individual specimen. Weeping matipo is hardy to cold and will grow in sun or shade. It will grow in quite poor soils but a good soil will make for a more encouraging rate of growth.

Propagate by seed.

Myrsine salicina
Toro

A small, erect-growing tree with attractive, long, narrow, shiny green, leathery leaves. It is usually no more than six or seven metres high. The leaves are bunched together at the ends of the branches and the pinkish flowers that occur in spring and the pink fruits that follow are borne on the bare stems just below the foliage. This attractive tree will grow in sun or shade. Where frosts are heavy it should be positioned where there is some shelter, such as beneath the overhang of tall trees.

Propagation is by seed, or cuttings of firm growth.

NOTHOFAGUS
Fagaceae

Nothofagus are the Southern Hemisphere beeches and are closely related to the genus *Fagus*, which contains the Northern Hemisphere beech trees. There are four *Nothofagus* species native to New Zealand, all endemic and occurring over much of the country. They are evergreen forest trees and are outstanding among the native flora. Beech forests often contain few other species of trees and shrubs, in contrast to other types of native forest, which generally contain a great mixture of flora. Anyone who has walked through a native beech forest will appreciate the beauty of their straight towering trunks and lacy foliage.

In the garden they make magnificent specimen trees but they are only suitable for large gardens and parks, although three species, *N. fusca*, *N. menziesii* and *N. truncata*, respond well to clipping and can be maintained as hedges. In large gardens and on farms they are worth considering for planting as a woodland instead of European trees such as birches and oaks, which are far more popular yet in many respects are not as handsome and often look out of place in the New Zealand environment. The native beech trees are cold hardy but must have shelter from salt winds. They will grow well in an average to moderately rich, well-drained garden soil.

Plants are easily raised from seed, which must be fresh.

Nothofagus fusca
Red beech

Young trees of this species have beautiful bright red

foliage during the winter months. It is highly ornamental and at one time was used extensively for floral work. The edges of the leaves are sharply toothed. In mature trees the foliage remains green throughout the year but in spring they are briefly deciduous, the old leaves falling off as the new foliage unfolds. This majestic tree is widely regarded as the most attractive of the native *Nothofagus* species. As a grand tree for a large garden, it is highly recommended, but bear in mind how tall it grows. In the wild this species is capable of reaching a height of 30 metres, although it is unusual to see it higher than 15 metres in cultivation. During its early years the rate of growth is quite rapid.

Nothofagus menziesii
Silver beech

The silver beech is a magnificent, wide-spreading, dome-shaped tree when grown in the open. When crowded in among other trees it assumes an upright form. The dark green leaves are smaller than the leaves of other beeches and are not shed in spring. The new spring foliage is light green and the silver beech is especially appealing at this season. The bark of young trees is an attractive silvery white; older trees have rough, flakey, grey-coloured bark. This is a handsome, tall specimen tree to grow where there is plenty of space.

Nothofagus solandri
Black beech

This handsome tree differs from the other species in that the oblong leaves are smaller, they lack toothed edges and are covered with a pale tomentum on their undersides.

In nature black beech is widespread throughout the South Island and the lower half of the North Island, often forming large tracts of forest in areas of mountain and hill country.

Nothofagus solandri var. *cliffortioides*
Mountain beech

Mountain beech is a smaller tree than *N. solandri*, seldom growing higher than 13 metres. This makes it more suitable than the other species for gardens where there is limited space. It also differs from *N. solandri* in that its leaves are small, oval shaped and pointed at the ends.

In nature it is found from East Cape southwards, often occurring in large numbers on mountain slopes where the soils are poor and the conditions are harsh. In these situations mountain beech is often stunted. Makes a graceful specimen tree in gardens.

Nothofagus truncata
Hard beech

This species is similar in appearance to *N. fusca*, but the foliage of young trees does not colour in winter, the leaves are smaller and the serrations on the leaf edges are blunter. It makes a grand specimen tree where there is lots of room. The common name refers to the fact that the wood of *N. truncata* is the hardest of the native beeches.

Its natural distribution is from Mangonui in the Far North to the upper areas of the South Island, from sea level to approximately 900 metres.

NOTOSPARTIUM
Papilionaceae

In this genus there are three species of distinctive, leafless shrubs, which occur in the South Island only. The two species mentioned are outstanding flowering shrubs but at present they are little known. A third species, *N. torulosum*, is quite attractive but suffers in comparison with the others. In nature they grow in rather light, sandy or shingly soils, but in gardens they seem to be happy in any well-drained soil. They should have full sun and seem to prefer a slightly dry situation, such as on a bank or in a raised garden. They are hardy to cold.

Propagation is by seed or cuttings.

Notospartium carmichaeliae

A slender, branching, leafless shrub, which will grow to a height of two to three metres in cultivation. In December and January the branches are covered with masses of bright pink, pea-shaped flowers, creating a spectacular sight. This is a very attractive shrub but at present it is hardly known to gardeners. When not in flower it looks rather like the well-known exotic brooms (*Genista* species) and combines well with other shrubs. The flower colour varies a little at times; especially good colour forms should be perpetuated by cuttings.

Notospartium glabrescens

This shrub is seldom more than two to three metres in height in cultivation although in the wild it sometimes attains the dimensions of a small tree. It is similar in its habit of growth to *N. carmichaeliae* but with a more pronounced weeping habit, and the display of bright mauve-pink flowers is generally considered to be even more striking. An outstanding shrub that is highly recommended.

OLEARIA
Compositae

Thirty-two species of *Olearia* are native to New Zealand. They vary in size from shrubs to small trees. Some are valuable for shelter and hedging, standing up well to wind and dry soils. *O. traversii* in particular is a most useful, fast-growing hedge plant, which will grow in a wide range of conditions including seaside sands. A few olearias, including some of those with the prettiest flowers such as *O. chathamica* and *O. semidentata* from the Chatham Islands, are unfortunately very difficult to grow, requiring cool, moist conditions. Because of their unreliability in cultivation they are not readily available, but one or two of the nurseries specialising in native plants do list them.

Most olearias are easily propagated by cuttings.

Olearia albida
Tanguru

A fast-growing, upright shrub or small tree with large, oblong, leathery leaves, which are dark green above and covered with white tomentum on the undersides. It is an excellent plant for shelter and hedging, standing up well to wind and tolerating dry conditions. Also makes an attractive background tree.

Olearia albida var. *angulata*

A smaller-growing tree than *O. albida*, with leathery, wavy-edged leaves. It is also an excellent shelter tree and, with its distinctive foliage, makes an attractive specimen tree. Stands up very well to wind and thrives in dry soils. It seems to be hardier to cold than *O. albida*, which sometimes suffers frost damage where frosts are heavy.

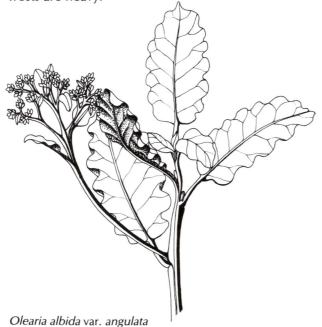

Olearia albida var. *angulata*

Olearia cheesemanii

Olearia cheesemanii

A large bushy shrub, with handsome, lance-shaped leaves and large heads of white daisy-like flowers in spring. It is very free flowering and it is often hard to see the foliage of a plant when it is in full bloom. A showy shrub for a sunny position. Grows to approximately two metres. Stands up well to wind. An easy, reliable plant to grow.

Olearia ilicifolia
Mountain holly

Forms a large spreading shrub with distinctive foliage, which is narrow and serrated and resembles that of holly. When well established it is free flowering and most attractive, and is covered with large heads of small, white daisy-like flowers in mid-summer. This species likes cool conditions and is usually more successful in colder districts. Plant it where there is shade from afternoon sun.

Olearia paniculata
Akiraho

A bushy shrub or small tree suitable for growing in dry soils. It has pretty, wavy-edged, leathery foliage, which is light green on top and covered with creamy grey tomentum on the undersides. The flowers are inconspicuous but they have a pleasant scent. It is cold hardy and makes an excellent drought- and wind-resistant hedge. A very well-drained soil is essential; damp soils are likely to cause the death of this tree. If allowed to develop naturally, it will form a small spreading tree with a slightly weeping habit, which, along with its distinctive foliage, makes it an attractive ornamental as well as a good shelter tree.

Olearia traversii
Chatham Island akeake

This tough coastal shrub is popular for hedging and shelter, especially in beach gardens, where it is able

Olearia traversii, Chatham Island akeake, growing in a farm paddock on the Chatham Islands

An untrimmed hedge of *Olearia traversii*, Chatham Island akeake

to make rapid growth in pure sand and to tolerate drought conditions. It makes a dense hedge up to two metres high, and with regular clipping can be kept quite narrow. The leaves are oval-oblong in shape, dark green on top and covered with finely matted, creamy-coloured hairs on the undersides. The creamy green flowers, produced in December, are insignificant.

When *O. traversii* is allowed to develop naturally, it becomes a small, upright tree five to ten metres high. Mature trees have very attractive light brown bark and develop considerable character as they age; it is a pity that untrimmed specimens are seen so seldom.

In nature *O. traversii* is found only on the Chatham Islands, where it grows near the sea.

Olearia traversii 'Variegata'

This variegated form has a creamy yellow margin to the leaves. It is not outstanding in comparison with many other variegated-foliage native trees and shrubs because the markings do not stand out boldly, but it is attractive nonetheless and has a certain novelty value. It is a little slower growing than the species but seems to be equally hardy.

OURISIA
Scrophulariaceae

There are approximately 10 species of *Ourisia* native to New Zealand and all are endemic. Most of the species occur in alpine regions. Plants are small with pretty white flowers, often with a touch of yellow in the throat. They are suitable for growing in rock gardens and require a gritty soil, lots of moisture throughout the year and shade from the afternoon sun. Obviously they are not plants for the casual gardener, but for the enthusiast who is prepared to take some care, they are most rewarding.

Ourisia cockayniana

This species is a creeping plant that roots down as it spreads and will form a large patch in gritty, constantly moist soil. It requires light shade. The white flowers are borne on 15-centimetre stems, and an established plant in full bloom is a delight.

Ourisia macrophylla

This handsome species is one of the easiest to grow in gardens. It has large leaves and long-stemmed flowers that occur in whorls, like candelabra primulas. There are several different varieties of this species, all of which are attractive. Grow it in a cool, lightly shaded spot.

Ourisia macrophylla

PACHYSTEGIA
Compositae

There is only one species belonging to the genus *Pachystegia*. *P. insignis*, Marlborough rock daisy, is an unusual native shrub that grows wild on dry, rocky outcrops and cliffs in Marlborough and North Canterbury. Its habitat extends from the coast (plants can be seen on the cliff faces beside the coast road north of Kaikoura) to well inland, up to an altitude of at least 900 metres. *P. insignis* var. *minor* is a smaller plant ideal for small gardens. Several distinctive forms of pachystegia have attracted considerable attention from botanists in recent times. Efforts are being made to bring them into cultivation and it is likely that they will be available from some nurseries in the future. One of the most striking of the forms is known as *Pachystegia* 'D'. It is low growing, with reddish flower stems and reddish fawn hairs on the bracts and on the undersides of the leaves.

Although pachystegias grow in remarkably barren and dry situations in the wild, they adapt well to varying conditions in gardens. They do not have to have dry or poor soils, but good drainage is important. Where the soil is heavy, they can be grown successfully in a raised garden. Failure of plants is often caused by poor drainage. Very humid conditions can also prove fatal. They are very hardy to cold and are not affected by salt winds. Pachystegias are suitable for a sunny shrub border and add a distinctive touch with both natives and exotics.

Pachystegias can be propagated by cuttings or seed. Seed will germinate readily but it must be fresh. Young seedlings should be protected from slugs and snails. Damping off of seedlings is likely if conditions are humid; they should be raised where there is adequate fresh air.

Pachystegia insignis
Marlborough rock daisy

A handsome, compact shrub, which will grow to a height of one metre in the garden. It has thick leathery leaves, green and smooth on the upper surface and covered with a dense mat of short, woolly, white hairs on the undersides. This layer of hair, or tomentum, extends around the edge of the upper surface, just far enough to produce a thin white margin around each leaf. Young leaves are covered completely with this protective tomentum, making a pleasant contrast with the shiny green mature leaves. From about the end of November to late December the bushes are covered with exquisitely formed white, daisy-like flowers, with prominent yellow centres. The light grey flower-buds on their long, sturdy stems look like perfectly formed, furry drum sticks and are most ornamental. They are prominent for some months before the flowers open.

Pachystegia insignis var. *minor*

Pachystegia insignis, Marlborough rock daisy

Pachystegia insignis var. *minor*

This is a much smaller plant than the species, seldom exceeding 30 centimetres in height and about 40 centimetres across. It is easily distinguished by its leaves, which are a darker shade of green, shinier, and do not have the white margin of hair. The flowers usually open several weeks later than those of *P. insignis*. This dwarf shrub is particularly good in rock gardens. It also excels on hot, dry banks and in crib walls.

PARAHEBE
Scrophulariaceae

Parahebe is an entirely New Zealand genus. The 11 species include several small, woody shrubs but most are low-growing or creeping plants that often form mats or cushions of foliage and are well suited to growing in rock gardens. The pretty flowers resemble those of the closely related hebes. These hardy, free-flowering plants are easy to grow if provided with a reasonably good, well-drained but not dry soil. They deserve to be better known as garden plants.

The simplest method of propagation is by cuttings.

Parahebe catarractae

The best forms of this plant are highly ornamental dwarf shrubs. The flowers are either white or purple. It grows to approximately 30 centimetres high, forming a rounded bush, and likes a reasonably rich, slightly moist soil. It will grow in sun or light shade; the latter is usually the most suitable where summers are long and hot. White-flowered forms stand out particularly well in shade.

Will grow readily from seed or cuttings. Selected colour forms should be propagated by cuttings.

Parahebe linifolia

A free-flowering, charming plant for growing in a rock garden or as a ground cover. It is a compact, much-branched little shrub, which grows to about 15 centimetres high. The small, freely produced flowers vary in colour from white to pink or pale blue. Flowering time is mid-summer. Performs best in a free-draining, slightly gritty soil. Water during dry summer weather.

Easy to grow from cuttings.

Parahebe linifolia 'Blue Skies'

An excellent form of *P. linifolia*, with larger flowers that are mauve-blue. It also seems to flower over a longer period than the species, often at several different times in addition to the main mid-summer period. Recommended.

Parahebe lyallii

A low-growing, spreading plant, usually less than 15 centimetres high, which roots down as it spreads. It varies in its habit of growth; the best forms are attractive cushions of small green leaves. The flowers, which are up to one centimetre in diameter, vary in colour from white to pink or pale blue with darker veining. Suitable for rock gardens or the front of a shrub border. Best in a soil that is not too dry.

Grows readily from cuttings.

PARATROPHIS
Moraceae

The three New Zealand species are endemic. One of these, *P. smithii*, is rare in cultivation and in nature is found on the Three Kings Islands only. It is a large shrub or small tree, up to five metres high. The other two species are small trees. A common characteristic of all three is the thick white sap that flows freely when the bark is cut, giving them the common name of milkwood. Early settlers used the sap as a substitute for milk in tea.

Paratrophis banksii
Towai, large-leaved milk tree

A handsome, small to medium-sized tree, which develops a spreading canopy of foliage. There are distinct juvenile and mature foliage forms. The juvenile leaves are deeply lobed and are most attractive; they often persist on the tree for some years after the adult foliage has developed. The creamy flowers are unremarkable. This is a tree well suited for planting as an individual specimen or for inclusion in a group of mixed trees and shrubs. It is moderately cold hardy. Where there are strong winds, it should be provided with some shelter. A deep, moist, well-drained, reasonably rich soil is ideal.

In nature it occurs in lowland forests from Mangonui in the Far North to the Marlborough Sounds.

Propagation is by seed or cuttings.

Paratrophis microphylla
Turepo, small-leaved milk tree

This tree is similar to *P. banksii* but its leaves are smaller. It lacks the ornamental appeal of the larger-leaved species and is not particularly significant for gardens.

It is cold hardy and occurs in lowland forests throughout New Zealand. Similar growing conditions to *P. banksii* are required.

Paratrophis microphylla 'Charles Devonshire'
Variegated turepo

The leaves of this attractive form display grey-green variegations and have a thin margin of cream. It is most distinctive and, as it is slow growing, can be accommodated in small gardens or in a container. It will grow in sun or light shade. The pretty foliage shows up particularly well against a dark background. It is rather rare, but plants are usually available from some of the specialist native plant nurseries. Requires a good soil and thorough watering during periods of drought.

It is propagated by cuttings.

PARSONSIA
Apocynaceae

There are two native species, both of which are endemic. They are interesting climbers and *P. heterophylla* in particular deserves to be far better known as a garden plant. They like similar conditions to clematis — good soil and a shaded root run — and the upper portion of the vine should be able to climb into full sun to produce flowers. They are hardy to cold.

Parsonsia heterophylla, New Zealand jasmine

Parsonsia capsularis

This slender climber has small, fragrant flowers, which vary in colour from white to yellow and red. The dark pink and red-flowered forms are particularly attractive but are little known and often hard to obtain from nurseries.

Good forms should be propagated by cuttings.

Parsonsia heterophylla
Kaihua, New Zealand jasmine

A vigorous, very ornamental twining climber, which can be grown on a trellis, trained along a fence or allowed to grow through a tall shrub or tree. The small, sweetly scented, creamy white flowers hang from the vines in thick clusters in spring and summer. Peak flowering time is usually in November and in a good season the blooms are so thick that most of the shiny green leaves are hidden. Seedling-raised plants undergo a juvenile foliage form that is quite distinct from that of adult plants. If plants are grown from cuttings taken from mature vines, the juvenile stage is by-passed and flowering will commence much sooner.

PASSIFLORA (TETRAPATHAEA)
Passifloraceae

The only New Zealand species, a slender climber, is endemic. It occurs in lowland forests as far south as Banks Peninsula.

Passiflora tetrandra, native passionfruit

Passiflora (Tetrapathaea) tetrandra
Kohia, native passionfruit

The native passionfruit will climb to a considerable height through tall trees or it can be trained to grow on a low fence. The flowers are small, white and sweetly scented, but the great attraction with this plant is the bright orange berries, which ripen in autumn. These are very ornamental and stand out well against the shiny green foliage. Because male and female flowers are borne on separate plants, vines of both sexes must be grown to produce the berries. The seeds within the berries are a popular item of diet for opossums, birds and possibly rats.

The native passionfruit should be planted so the roots are in cool shade yet the vine can grow up into the sun to flower. In a reasonably rich soil it grows quickly.

Plants can be propagated from seed or cuttings. The latter method allows for easy selection of male and female plants.

PENNANTIA
Icacinaceae

The two native species of *Pennantia* are endemic. One, *P. baylisiana*, occurs only on Great King Island

of the Three Kings Islands and is rarely seen in cultivation. It is a small tree with large glossy foliage. The other species, *P. corymbosa*, is widespread, occurring over much of the North Island from Kaitaia southwards and throughout the South Island.

Pennantia corymbosa
Kaikomako

A small tree of slender habit, sometimes growing as tall as 10 metres but usually less. Trees grown from seed pass through a juvenile stage characterised by dense, interlacing branches. At its best this stage is uninteresting. The adult form, which takes some years to develop, is quite different. The mature tree is elegant, with handsome, dark green foliage and beautiful creamy white, fragrant flowers, which are often produced so freely that the foliage is almost obscured. Flowering time is from early to late summer. The small black fruits attract native birds.

Kaikomako is an attractive specimen tree that, thanks to its slender form, can be accommodated in quite small gardens. It should be planted in a good moist soil. Hardy to cold. The juvenile stage can be bypassed if trees are propagated from cuttings taken from adult trees. Kaikomako was a favourite firewood of the Maori.

PERSOONIA
Proteaceae

One endemic species of *Persoonia* occurs in New Zealand. The other 60 or so species in the genus are confined to Australia.

Persoonia toru
Toru

With its upright, bushy habit of growth and dark green, narrow, shiny, leathery leaves, this tree is a handsome subject for small gardens. The yellow-brown flowers are sweetly scented. Toru will grow in most garden soils providing there is good drainage. A sunny situation will encourage the most handsome form. It seems to be cold hardy in most lowland districts.

Its natural distribution is in the upper North Island, where it grows in scrubland and forest from sea level to approximately 850 metres.

The simplest method of propagation is from seed.

PHEBALIUM
Rutaceae

One endemic species occurs in New Zealand; most of the other 30 or more species are native to Australia.

Phebalium nudum
Mairehau

A small, ornamental shrub, which is surprisingly rare in cultivation. It seldom grows higher than one metre in gardens and has a bushy habit. The narrow leaves are an attractive green-brown colour and have an agreeable fragrance. In spring pretty white, star-shaped, sweetly scented flowers are produced on the tips of the branches. This is an interesting shrub for planting in the foreground of a shrub border. It does best in partial shade and should have good soil that does not dry out. Water thoroughly during periods of dry weather. It is hardy to cold. An occasional pruning will maintain a compact habit of growth.

Propagate by cuttings.

PHORMIUM
Agavaceae

Phormium, or flax, are among the best-known native plants and are easily recognised by their distinctive form. They have always provided a valuable source of leaves and fibre for Maori weaving. There are only two species in the genus. One of these, *P. cookianum*, is confined to this country. The other, *P. tenax*, is found on Norfolk Island as well as throughout New Zealand. One of the fascinating things about these plants is their versatility. They will grow in all sorts of soils and climates (they are quite hardy to cold) without any special attention.

In recent years many new flaxes with brightly coloured foliage have become available, thanks to the efforts of the plant hybridisers. Some of these are among the most striking of all our native plants. Most flaxes will grow in gardens with little attention apart from an occasional trimming of the old leaves, although some of the more vigorous ones will need dividing and replanting after a time.

To propagate flaxes, simply divide them in winter and replant. Each strong fan will grow. It pays to cut off most of the foliage when carrying out this operation.

Flaxes are sometimes attacked by the leaf-cutting flax moth, which feeds at night and makes big vee-shaped holes in the edges of the leaves. A white scale also affects flaxes at times. Both these pests are relatively simple to control by spraying with an insecticide, preferably at the first sign of their presence.

Flaxes are marvellous for creating a bold tropical look in a garden. They combine well with all sorts of shrubs, both native and exotic, and the variety of colours, sizes and forms means that there are flaxes for most situations. When combined with bold-foliaged native trees and shrubs such as some of the *Pseudopanax*, cabbage trees (*Cordyline*), *Meryta sinclairii*, tree ferns or *Griselinia lucida*, the result is striking. Flaxes are also superb plants to use as a focal point among low-growing ground covers, including natives such as *Pimelea prostrata*, some of the *Coprosma* species and cultivars, *Acaena* species and others. The following list of *Phormium* cultivars does not include every one that is obtainable but it attempts to give some description of those that are most popular. No doubt the future will see many new and worthwhile flaxes become available.

Phormium 'Centennial Fanfare'

An upright flax with dark leaves and a margin of bright red. This highly ornamental cultivar was released in 1982 to coincide with the centennial of Tauranga. Grows to a height of 1.5 metres.

Phormium cookianum
Mountain flax, wharariki

Despite the name mountain flax, this species is found in the wild along the coast as well as in lower mountain regions. It occurs in the North and South Islands and Stewart Island. It is a smaller plant than *P. tenax*, growing one to 1.5 metres high, and is distinguished by its drooping and twisted seed-pods, unlike those of *P. tenax*, which are held erect. The foliage of *P. cookianum* is usually weeping, and it is a graceful plant well suited to planting in gardens and for use in public landscaping. It is an interesting flax to plant alongside one of the deep bronze cultivars, its shiny green leaves making an interesting foil to the darker-coloured foliage.

Phormium cookianum flowers

Phormium cookianum 'Purpureum'

A purple-foliage form of *P. cookianum*, with the same attractive habit of growth and dimensions, differing only in the foliage colour.

Phormium cookianum 'Tricolor'

This variegated flax has been a favourite for many years and despite the numerous new cultivars it

Phormium cookianum 'Tricolor' growing among assorted native plants including hebes, *Coprosma repens* 'Silver Queen', ratas and *Griselinia lucida*.

remains one of the best. It has a beautiful weeping habit and the long leaves, which measure from one to 1.5 metres, are green with cream stripes and a prominent red margin. This is one of the tidiest flaxes; the old leaves do not need to be trimmed as often as most cultivars and the foliage always looks fresh. The weeping habit makes it a good subject for planting beside water or to grow on a bank. It will grow in light shade as well as in the open.

Phormium 'Cream Delight'

A beautiful variegated flax with cream-and-green leaves and a weeping habit of growth. Looks especially striking in a slightly raised garden or on a bank so its graceful form is shown off to advantage.

Phormium 'Dark Delight'

The deep maroon foliage and upright habit of this cultivar make it a striking plant. Marvellous for contrasting with light-coloured buildings or foliage. Grows to 1.5 metres.

Phormium 'Dazzler'

One of the smaller flaxes and one of the most colourful. The leaves are a deep bronze-maroon with prominent scarlet stripes. It is quite small, seldom reaching a height of more than 75 centimetres, and has an arching habit of growth. Although this flax will grow in widely varying conditions including poor

Phormium 'Dazzler'

Phormium 'Maori Sunrise'

An attractive flax of upright habit. The leaves are reddish pink with a bronze margin.

Phormium 'Rubrum'

A compact flax, usually less than one metre high, with dark bronze-purple foliage. It is a distinctive cultivar well suited to small gardens and makes a nice contrast in colour and form among low-growing green- or yellow-leaved shrubs. This flax has remained popular for more than half a century, quite an achievement considering the number of attractive new cultivars that have become available over the last decade or so.

Phormium 'Smiling Morn'

This was one of the first of the artificial hybrid flaxes with coloured foliage, raised by Mr W. B. Brockie when he was at the Christchurch Botanic Gardens. It is an attractive weeping flax with pink and creamy yellow markings. The colouring is more subtle than many of the variegated flaxes, which might explain why this cultivar is not better known. It is a good garden plant, growing to about a metre high, not too vigorous and easily managed.

Phormium 'Sundowner'

A brightly coloured, upright flax that will grow to a height of 1.5 metres. The leaves are bronze-green with a broad margin of deep pink and crimson. The colouring is good year round but especially bright on new growth. This is a striking plant for bold effect in the garden and it is also one of the best flaxes for growing in a large container.

Phormium 'Sunset'

The narrow leaves of this distinctive cultivar display pale orange markings. It will grow to a height of 1.5 metres. A popular flax for floral work.

soils, it develops its best colour in a good, moist soil. Its compact habit makes it ideal for small gardens.

Phormium 'Duet'

A small flax, usually no higher than 75 centimetres. The erect leaves are cream and light green. While not one of the more spectacular cultivars, it is still good as a contrast plant and its size makes it useful for small gardens.

Phormium 'Emerald Gem'

A compact, small flax with bright green foliage. In massed plantings it forms a maintenance-saving ground cover. Also good for small gardens where the larger flaxes may take up too much room.

Phormium 'Maori Maiden'

A striking flax with narrow, arching leaves, which are apricot-red with bronze margins. Grows to approximately one metre.

Phormium 'Maori Queen'

An upright flax, growing to a height of about one metre, with bronze leaves edged with pink or red.

Phormium 'Maori Sunrise'. The ground cover in the foreground is *Coprosma* 'Kirkii'.

Phormium 'Surfer'

A dwarf flax, up to 45 centimetres high, with green and brown leaves. It is useful for rock gardens and for planting where there is not room for larger flaxes. Makes an interesting contrast among dwarf native shrubs.

Phormium tenax
New Zealand flax, harakeke

Occurring throughout New Zealand, *P. tenax* is distinguished by its erect habit and its leaves, which are usually more rigid than those of *P. cookianum.* It grows in all sorts of situations in the wild, from wind-swept hillsides to swamps and from lower mountain regions to the coast. In the garden it is useful as a background plant and for growing in wet ground where the conditions suit few other plants, yet it is equally at home in any good garden soil or in the dry sands of a beach garden. *P. tenax* also makes an effective low hedge or shelter planting, proving especially useful for exposed sites and dry soils.

Phormium tenax 'Purpureum'

A very erect flax, 1.5 to two metres high, with stiff, bronze-purple leaves. Interesting to contrast with rounded plant forms. Good for landscaping. Strong growing.

Phormium tenax 'Radiance'

This stiffly upright flax is not as colourful as some of the modern hybrids but it has a distinctive form and is strong growing and tidy. The leaves are striped green and light yellow, with the yellow dominant. It is a good flax for growing beside a lawn, for few leaves ever hang down and get in the way of mowers, unlike some of those with drooping foliage, which require frequent trimming to keep them away from mower blades. Occasionally it is seen as a hedge and is most attractive when used in this way.

Phormium 'Yellow Wave'

Phormium 'Williamsii Variegata'

Phormium tenax 'Williamsii Variegatum'

A beautiful and dramatic flax, the wide green leaves displaying broad bands of creamy yellow. It is erect growing, well over two metres high, and forms bold clumps. This flax is too large for small gardens but it could be grown as a feature plant in a comparatively small space. Wherever it is grown it arouses interest for it is striking and distinct from most other flaxes. Sometimes it is confused with *P. tenax* 'Radiance' but it is much larger and more handsome. It does best in a good, moist soil.

Phormium 'Thumbelina'

A dwarf flax, seldom more than 35 centimetres high, with very narrow, purple-bronze leaves. It is particularly useful for small gardens. Distinctive when mass planted as a ground cover or among ground-cover shrubs or ornamental native tussocks such as some of the *Carex* species.

Phormium 'Tom Thumb'

This dwarf flax has narrow, bronze-green foliage margined with brown. It is similar in size to *P.* 'Thumbelina' and can be used in the same way.

Phormium 'Yellow Wave'

One of the most popular coloured flaxes, it has a drooping habit that is most pleasing in the garden. The leaves are light green with a broad central stripe of yellow. It is strong growing, and plants should be divided and replanted after a time. A lovely flax to grow alongside shrubs and small trees of upright habit. Will reach a height of 1.5 metres.

PHYLLOCLADUS
Podocarpaceae

The three species of *Phyllocladus* that occur in New Zealand are endemic. They are unique trees, characterised by their whorled branches and the flattened, expanded stems, known as phylloclades, which function as leaves. In the garden they make distinctive and highly ornamental specimen trees and it is surprising that they are not grown more widely.

They are best propagated by seed.

Phyllocladus alpinus
Mountain toa toa

A slow-growing shrub or small tree with smaller phylloclades than the other species. It is notable for the vivid red cones. A reasonably rich, moist soil is ideal. Hardy to cold

Phyllocladus glaucus
Toa toa

Forms a steeply pyramidal tree, eventually reaching a height of eight to 10 metres, occasionally more. The phylloclades of this species are thick and leathery and shaped like a wedge, with finely toothed edges. It is a striking tree and makes a handsome specimen. It is slow growing, which might explain why it is not seen more often in gardens, but this means that it can be accommodated in small gardens with ease. Toa toa should have good soil and be grown in the open so that its form can develop unhindered by other trees. It is hardy to cold. Should have protection from strong winds.

Occurs naturally in native forests of the upper North Island.

Phyllocladus trichomanoides
Tanekaha, celery pine

The phylloclades of this species are arranged in a pattern that resembles a leaf of celery, thus the common name celery pine. It is a striking tree that is marvellous as a specimen. It will grow in sun or shade, but an open situation where it can display its graceful pyramidal form fully and where its development is not affected by encroaching trees is the most suitable. It is a moderately fast-growing tree with an eventual height of eight to 10 metres. Hardy to cold. Should have good soil and shelter from wind on exposed sites.

PIMELEA
Thymelaeaceae

There are about 20 species of *Pimelea* native to New Zealand. Only one, *P. prostrata*, is at all well known as a garden plant, but several more deserve to be better known.

Propagation is by cuttings of firm tip growth.

Pimelea arenaria
Sand daphne

This pretty, prostrate shrub with grey leaves and hairy stems grows in the wild on top of sand dunes, where it forms thick cushions and helps to prevent erosion. It requires a sunny situation and excellent drainage and is excellent for beach gardens or the top of a sun-baked bank or wall. It produces attractive white flowers in spring and summer.

Propagate by cuttings. Plants can be obtained from specialist nurseries.

Pimelea prostrata

Pimelea longifolia
Taranga, New Zealand daphne

This delightful shrub has large heads of white, scented flowers. It forms an upright bush, one to 1.5 metres high, with dark green, lance-shaped leaves. It requires a well-drained but not too dry soil and an open, sunny situation.

Pimelea prostrata

A prostrate, spreading shrub with attractive grey foliage and small white flowers. It is ideal as a ground cover and weed suppressant, and for planting in crib walls and on banks. Looks marvellous spilling over a rock wall or spreading over the ground in front of shrubs. The small grey foliage is an excellent foil for colourful flowers or leaves and also looks delightful in association with small native shrubs such as hebes. As an underplanting to variegated flaxes with pink foliage it is superb. It is also popular for use in large rock gardens and for planting in between paving stones or as a contrast plant at the base of a large rock. *P. prostrata* is easy to grow in virtually any soil type providing there is good drainage. It does best in sun.

PISONIA
Nyctaginaceae

One species of this small genus occurs in New Zealand. It is a handsome tree but is not particularly popular for gardens. However, there is a variegated form with striking foliage, a magnificent shrub for growing in a mild climate.

Pisonia brunoniana (Heimerliodendron brunonianum)
Parapara

A big, bushy shrub or small tree with very large, green leaves. It is useful for imparting a tropical atmosphere to gardens but is only suitable for mild districts as it is frost tender. The plain-leaved species is rather notorious for its ability to ensnare small birds such as waxeyes and fantails. This occurs because the long, narrow, green fruits secrete a sticky substance that traps insects. These attract the birds and smaller kinds often become stuck to the fruits, with fatal results. (One of my most vivid childhood memories is of seeing a large parapara with dead birds attached in an old garden.) It is hardly surprising, therefore, that many people refuse to grow parapara.

Pisonia brunoniana 'Variegata'

This magnificent variegated-foliage form is less vigorous than the plain-leaved species, takes longer to produce flowers and seems to have fewer of them,

Pisonia brunoniana 'Variegata'

but it is a striking plant. The large leaves of this big shrub are beautifully marked with splashes of cream and several shades of green, creating a varied pattern that looks as if it has been hand painted. Further interest is added by the new growth, which displays pink tints.

P. brunoniana 'Variegata' should be grown in a reasonably rich, well-drained soil. A shaded situation is regarded as ideal as the foliage sometimes burns in full sun. Where there are even light frosts some overhead protection (overhanging trees or eaves) is necessary. It does extremely well beneath tall, light-foliaged trees providing the conditions are not too dry or poor. Some shelter is necessary; if planted in a windy spot the tops of the branches are inclined to snap off.

This plant is outstanding for landscaping in mild areas. Whether brightening a dark corner of a garden or providing a brilliant contrast to bold-foliaged natives such as puka (*Meryta sinclairii*), it adds a distinctive note that few other shrubs can match. The foliage stands out dramatically against a dark shadowy background or against the warm tones of lightly stained timber. *P. brunoniana* 'Variegata' grows well in containers and makes a grand specimen in a large tub on a patio or in a courtyard. It is also a most attractive subject for growing as a house plant and in conservatories and glasshouses.

Propagation is by cuttings. The best time to take these is in late summer and autumn.

PITTOSPORUM
Pittosporaceae

Among the 26 species of *Pittosporum* that occur in New Zealand are some of our most ornamental and useful native trees and shrubs. Most are fast growing, and species such as *P. crassifolium* and *P. eugenioides* make reliable wind- and drought-resistant hedges and shelter trees as well as being sufficiently ornamental to deserve a place in the garden as individual specimens. *P. crassifolium* is also noted for its ability to grow beneath taller trees where the shady and often dry conditions suit few plants. A number of pittosporums are beautiful background trees, and some of the variegated-foliage cultivars are distinctive and colourful. Many are useful for floral work. The flowers of most species are not particularly significant but are still attractive and some are pleasantly fragrant. Most of the species are cold hardy and will grow readily in most soil types providing there is good drainage.

Propagation of the species is usually by seed. The

Pittosporum crassifolium, karo

variegated-foliage cultivars are generally raised from cuttings.

Pittosporum crassifolium
Karo

Karo is a small, erect tree, which can grow as tall as five metres. It is by nature a tree of the coast and is well equipped to handle the harsh conditions of exposed coastal sites. Sand, drought and salt-laden winds are no problem for this tough but handsome native. It responds well to trimming and is often used as a hedge, particularly in coastal areas, but it is also suitable for inland gardens. Old specimens can be cut hard back if desired and they will quickly shoot into new bushy growth. But its abilities as a hedge should not be allowed to obscure its attractions as a specimen tree, for it is quite handsome when allowed to develop its natural form. It has a surprising ability to grow in shade and is most useful for growing as a ground-draught break beneath tall trees. The leaves of karo are thick and leathery, shiny green on top and pale grey on the undersides, which are covered with a layer of tomentum. The flowers are dark red and are produced on the tips of the branches during spring. They are pleasantly scented, the fragrance being most obvious in the evening. The rounded seed-capsules are surprisingly large and are quite ornamental. They are covered by a thin layer of greyish white tomentum, which adds to their appeal. When ripe they split open to reveal shiny, black, sticky seeds.

Karo is easy to raise from seed and often self-sows freely. Seedlings transplant readily providing they are lifted during winter while small.

Pittosporum crassifolium berries

Pittosporum crassifolium 'Variegatum'

This most attractive cultivar has grey-green foliage with a cream margin. It has the same bushy, upright habit as the species but is much slower growing. A handsome small tree, it will grow in sun or shade and stands up well to wind. Young plants may require protection from heavy frosts but once established should be cold hardy in most districts.

Propagation by cuttings is usually difficult and it may be necessary to graft plants onto seedlings of the species.

Pittosporum eugenioides
Tarata, lemonwood

Tarata is a fast-growing, small tree, which is popular for shelter and hedging. It also makes a most attractive specimen or background tree. Young trees have a conical shape and are clothed with foliage to the ground. Mature trees develop a rounded crown and a sturdy trunk that is clear of branches. The leaves of tarata are an attractive light green colour. When crushed they give off a strong smell of lemon. The yellow flowers are produced in large clusters on the ends of the branches. They are highly ornamental and have a strong fragrance of honey. The Maori people mixed the flowers with fat to annoint their bodies. Tarata is normally an accommodating tree, growing with ease in most soil types and situations, but it is not at home in very exposed beach gardens. *P. crassifolium* is a better choice where shelter from salt winds is desired.

Pittosporum eugenioides 'Variegatum'

The leaves of this outstanding cultivar are light green with an irregular cream margin. In other respects it is identical to the plain green-leaved species. It is a most attractive subject for planting on a boundary or as an individual specimen in all sorts of situations. On occasion it is seen as a street tree and it could be used more often for this purpose.

Pittosporum crassifolium 'Variegatum'

Pittosporum eugenioides

Pittosporum eugenioides 'Variegatum'

Pittosporum 'Garnettii'

This hardy, vigorous cultivar is of hybrid origin. The leaves are grey-green with an irregular margin of white. During winter the white margins are often flushed with pink. It grows to approximately three metres and will succeed in either full sun or light shade. It is an old favourite that has featured in New Zealand gardens for years.

Pittosporum ralphii

A small spreading tree with large, rather narrow, oblong-shaped leaves and dark red flowers. It bears a strong resemblance to *P. crassifolium* but has a more rounded habit and larger, lighter green leaves. *P. ralphii* is hardy to cold and stands up well to wind. Most soil types are suitable, providing there is good drainage, and it will grow in sun or shade. Grows with ease in poor, dry soils. An excellent tree for shelter but also attractive enough to grow as a specimen. It succeeds near the coast, but where conditions are very exposed the remarkably tough *P. crassifolium* is a better choice.

Pittosporum ralphii 'Variegatum'

This is an elegant variegated shrub with grey-green foliage surrounded by an irregular cream margin. It will grow in sun or shade, but the foliage colour seems to show up better in low light. It is considerably slower growing than the plain-leaved species and is well suited to small gardens.

Pittosporum tenuifolium
Kohuhu

Kohuhu is a hardy tree with small, shiny, green leaves, which are attractive all year round. During spring it has small, dark red flowers, the pleasant scent of which is strongest in the evenings. The bark is usually dark grey or almost black. This small hardy tree is often grown as a shelter or background tree and also makes a good hedge. It is a variable species and a number of cultivars with attractive foliage have arisen from it. Many of these are outstanding garden shrubs with beautiful fine foliage. They are marvellous for combining with bold-foliage trees and shrubs such as *Meryta sinclairii, Griselinia lucida, Pseudopanax* and others. They also combine well with many exotics; cultivars with cream and green colourings look superb among camellias, for instance. *P. tenuifolium* cultivars are seldom seen as clipped specimens but when treated in this way can be striking. Their potential as ornamental hedges is great but as yet is little realised.

New cultivars come onto the market from time to time so the following list is unlikely to be complete, but it does contain those that have remained popular for some time or look particularly promising. Keep an eye out for good new cultivars in the future.

Pittosporum tenuifolium 'James Stirling'

The small, rounded leaves of this cultivar are a light, silvery grey-green. It has a dainty look about it and is an attractive, upright-growing foliage tree. Makes an attractive combination with other trees and shrubs with colourful or bold foliage. For example, it stands out well when seen alongside *Metrosideros kermadecensis* 'Variegata'. It was named for James Stirling, who was New Zealand's first television gardening personality and at one time was in charge of Government House grounds in Wellington. Apparently this cultivar originated in his Wellington garden. It is not as popular as it was and it seems likely that it will be superseded by the newer cultivars.

Pittosporum tenuifolium 'Deborah'

Forms a large shrub or small tree up to three metres tall. The small foliage is light grey-green with an irregular margin of cream flushed with pink. Old leaves are often flushed with pink all over. A pretty foliage shrub.

Pittosporum tenuifolium 'Irene Patterson'

This is a handsome foliage shrub, with white leaves speckled with green and grey-green. During winter

A clipped specimen of *Pittosporum tenuifolium* 'Mellow Yellow'

the foliage often has a pink tinge. Makes a large, bushy shrub for a mixed planting, providing interesting contrast.

Pittosporum tenuifolium 'Katie'

A dainty shrub with small, light green leaves margined with white. Similar to *P. tenuifolium* 'Stirling Silver' but the foliage is slightly larger and the green portion of the leaves is a paler shade.

Pittosporum tenuifolium 'Mellow Yellow'

The beautiful small foliage is mostly yellow with a slim margin of green. The black stems make a striking contrast. An outstanding foliage shrub.

Pittosporum tenuifolium 'Stirling Gold'

Similar to *P. tenuifolium* 'James Stirling' but the leaves display green and pale yellow variegations.

Pittosporum tenuifolium 'Stirling Silver'

The dainty grey-green leaves have a thin margin of white. The foliage colour stands out against the black stems. A striking new cultivar.

Pittosporum tenuifolium 'Sunburst'

This cultivar has larger foliage than the dainty *P. tenuifolium* 'Stirling Silver'. The leaves have a bold central splash of pale yellow surrounded by an irregular margin of light green. The overall effect is of pale yellow foliage. Has an open habit. Most attractive.

Pittosporum tenuifolium 'Sunburst'

Pittosporum tenuifolium 'Yellow Waves'

One of the larger-leaved *P. tenuifolium* cultivars. The recurved, wavy-edged leaves are pale yellow with an irregular, thin margin of dark green. The old leaves are plain green. Sometimes develops interesting colour variations. Also shows a tendency to revert to plain green on occasion; when this happens such growths should be cut out as soon as they are noticed.

PLAGIANTHUS
Malvaceae

The two native species of *Plagianthus* are endemic. They are very different, one being a tall deciduous tree of ornamental value, the other a twiggy shrub of the coast useful for hedging in difficult conditions.

Plagianthus betulinus (P. regius)
Manatu, riverbank ribbonwood

The common name of this deciduous tree alludes to its preference for growing on flood plains of streams and rivers in high-rainfall areas. It occurs over much of the country, including Stewart Island and the Chathams. With an ultimate height of 10 to 15 metres, this is the largest deciduous tree native to New Zealand. On mature trees the new, bright green spring foliage is most attractive, as is the form, which is characterised by an open habit, a stout trunk and thick, wide-spreading branches.

In their juvenile stage young trees are bushy and the branches are close set and interlacing. This habit often persists low down on mature trees, and in the garden these branches should be removed for the sake of appearance. Male and female flowers are borne on separate trees. Those of the male are more attractive, being larger and a lighter shade of green. Manatu is able to withstand strong winds, unlike so many deciduous trees, which need sheltered situations. It will grow in most soil types but is best in a reasonably rich loam.

Ideally, propagation should be by cuttings taken from male trees.

Plagianthus divaricatus
Maritime ribbonwood

The maritime or salt-water ribbonwood is a twiggy, dark-stemmed, deciduous shrub with few leaves. The small flowers are sweetly scented. It rates rather poorly as an ornamental but as a hedge for swampy ground near the sea it has few equals, for it combines the unusual abilities of being salt-wind resistant and tolerant of wet soils. This exceptionally tough shrub grows to a height of approximately two metres.

It can be propagated by seed or cuttings. Plants are obtainable from some specialist native plant nurseries.

PLANCHONELLA
Sapotaceae

There are about a hundred species belonging to the genus *Planchonella* but only one, a handsome, frost-tender tree, is native to New Zealand. It occurs on the coast of the upper North Island, from North Cape to Tolaga Bay in the east, and as far south as Manukau harbour on the west coast.

Planchonella novo-zelandica
Tawapou

Forms a dense, closely branched, upright tree, which seldom reaches a height of more than seven metres. The oval-shaped leaves are dark green and glossy and patterned with a network of veins. The flowers are tiny, but the orange berries that follow are quite large and are very showy. Each berry contains up to four hard, shiny seeds. The Maori used to polish the seeds and make them into necklaces.

Tawapou is not hardy to cold, and anything more than a slight frost usually causes damage. Where the climate is mild, it can be grown in the open as a handsome tree, either on its own or in combination with other natives. Where light to moderate frosts are experienced, it can be grown in a sheltered situation, such as on the edge of a grove of tall trees. Combines well with trees that have contrasting foliage. It should have a reasonably rich soil.

Plants can be raised from seed.

PODOCARPUS
Podocarpaceae

The seven native *Podocarpus* species are all endemic. They range from tall trees suitable as specimens for large gardens to dwarf shrubs that can be accommodated in nearly every garden. Some species deserve more attention from gardeners, particularly *P. dacrydioides*, which is a magnificent specimen tree. Unfortunately it has an unattractive juvenile stage but this can be overcome if plants are raised from cuttings taken from trees that have outgrown this form. Also outstanding is the golden-foliage form of the totara, *P. totara* 'Aurea'. *Podocarpus* are very hardy to cold and easy to grow.

They can be propagated by seed or cuttings.

Podocarpus acutifolius
Needle-leaved totara

If allowed to develop naturally, *P. acutifolius* forms a small tree up to 15 metres in height, with an open habit of growth. If trimmed it makes a compact shrub. The leaves are straight and needle pointed. If grown in full sun the foliage will often take on an attractive golden yellow colour, although the degree of colour does vary in different forms. As a hedge plant it should be excellent yet it seems to be untried for this purpose. It is easy to grow and hardy to cold. Rarely seen in gardens.

Podocarpus (now *Dacrycarpus*) dacrydioides
Kahikatea, white pine

Common from lowland to hill forests throughout New Zealand, particularly in swampy ground, where it is often the dominant species. This is the tallest native tree but in gardens it is unusual for specimens to attain a height of more than nine to 10 metres. It makes a striking tree when mature, with its erect, narrowly pyramidal habit and dark green foliage. Kahikatea is quite happy in any reasonably moist soil but is particularly useful for growing in wet soils where few trees will survive; it will even grow under water.

Kahikatea has a juvenile stage of growth that is not nearly as attractive as the mature form. Unfortunately, this immature form persists for some years before the handsome, cypress-like, fastigiate, adult form is assumed. However, if trees are propagated from cuttings taken from mature kahikatea, the uninteresting juvenile stage is bypassed.

The berries of kahikatea are a favourite food of the native pigeon and where there are mature trees these big birds are often seen eating their fill. The pre-European Maori used to set pigeon snares in kahikatea trees. The great height of the trees meant that setting the snares was often a dangerous task and on occasion an intrepid fowler would fall to his death, giving rise to the saying that those who set snares in the kahikatea were 'food for roots'. The berries were also gathered in baskets, washed and eaten raw.

Podocarpus ferrugineus
Miro

This small tree resembles the common yew but is more attractive because of its graceful, often weeping branchlets. Ideally, it should have a rich soil that does not dry out, but it will also grow in quite dry soils. A slightly shaded position is preferred. The large red berries of miro are highly ornamental, standing out against the dark green foliage, but as these trees are dioecious (male and female flowers are on separate plants), the berries will only occur when both sexes are growing nearby. Miro responds well to clipping and can be kept to a desired height by this means.

Podocarpus hallii
Hall's totara, thin-bark totara

This tree is very similar to *P. totara*, but is distinguished by its thin, papery bark and larger foliage. It is smaller than *P. totara*, seldom growing higher than five metres in cultivation and making a good specimen tree. It is also suitable for hedging, although it is seldom used for this purpose. It is extremely cold hardy and grows readily in gardens.

Podocarpus nivalis
Mountain totara

This species varies in its habit from a prostrate, spreading ground cover to a small, erect shrub up to a metre high. It bears a strong resemblance to *P. totara* but is smaller in all its parts and the foliage is blunt, rather than pointed and prickly. The

Podocarpus dacrydioides, kahikatea

Podocarpus nivalis, mountain totara

Podocarpus totara 'Aurea'

Podocarpus totara 'Aurea' as a hedge

Podocarpus totara
Totara

A handsome specimen tree for larger gardens. It grows with ease in virtually any soil type and is hardy to cold and wind, but it does not grow readily in exposed coastal gardens. Young totaras have foliage to ground level; as they mature they assume the true form of a bare trunk and rounded head of dark-green foliage. Although mature totara grow to a considerable height in the wild, it is unusual for specimens in cultivation to exceed nine or 10 metres.

The brownish bark of totara is an attractive feature; in old trees the bark is usually shed in long, thick strips, which were used by the Maori for roofing, to make baskets for carrying food and splints for broken limbs.

Totara trees are very long lived, and some specimens in the wild are estimated to be 800 or more years old. The massive trunks of mature totaras were used to make the famous Maori war canoes, the timber being ideal for this purpose as it is strong, light, and durable in water.

Totara responds well to clipping, providing such treatment is started at a reasonably early age. This means that totaras can be kept to a low height if desired. Totara also makes an extremely good hedge, forming a dense barrier of close-knit foliage when clipped regularly.

Podocarpus totara 'Aurea'
Golden totara

A beautiful, golden yellow cultivar of totara. This desirable native must be one of the finest foliage trees there is. It makes a striking specimen, and a group of several trees, spaced far enough apart so that they can develop without becoming crowded, can look most impressive. *P. totara* 'Aurea' is slower growing than the species, which makes it easier to accommodate in small gardens. Where space is at a premium, it can be kept compact by trimming. As a hedge, it has all the good qualities of the species, as well

mountain totara is extremely hardy to cold and is very easy to grow in any reasonable garden soil. The prostrate form is of interest for rock gardens and on banks and walls. The upright form is an attractive foliage shrub, useful as a contrast to brighter-coloured foliage and flowers. It is also of interest as a dwarf hedge. When male and female plants are present, fleshy, bright red fruits are produced.

Propagate by cuttings.

Podocarpus spicatus
Matai, black pine

This tree is similar to *P. ferrugineus* but it undergoes an unattractive, twiggy juvenile stage before taking on the handsome adult foliage. The juvenile stage can, as with the kahikatea, be avoided by taking cuttings from adult trees. The main advantage of this species over *P. ferrugineus* is its greater ability to tolerate dry and poor soils.

Matai timber is noted for its durability, strength and attractive grain. Thomas Kirk, the highly regarded, nineteenth-century botanist, recorded that the watery portion of the sap sometimes accumulates in cavities during the growing season and provides a refreshing beverage.

as its bright foliage colour, which makes it an exceptional hedging plant.

There is a little-known form of totara with attractive weeping foliage. It is hard to obtain but is sometimes available from nurseries specialising in native plants. Also of interest is *P. totara* 'Prostrata', a prostrate-growing form, which at the time of writing was listed by only one native plant nursery (Titan Nurseries, Hawera).

POMADERRIS
Rhamnaceae

Seven species of *Pomaderris* are native to New Zealand but only two are widely grown as garden plants. Of these *P. kumeraho* is of most interest to gardeners.

Pomaderris apetala
Tainui

Tainui is quick growing, with an upright habit and narrow, wrinkled, rough-textured leaves, which have small hairs on the undersides. The greenish yellow flowers are unspectacular and tainui is seldom cultivated purely as an ornamental. It is, however, a reliable, extremely tough shelter plant that withstands wind and drought and is unaffected by quite heavy frosts. As a coastal hedge it is a good choice, although in very exposed situations other natives such as pohutukawa (*Metrosideros excelsa*), taupata (*Coprosma repens*) or broadleaf (*Griselinia littoralis*) should be planted. It can reach a height of five metres, but when grown as a hedge it will require frequent trimming to keep it neat and tidy.

Pomaderris kumeraho
Kumarahou, golden tainui

When in full flower in spring kumarahou is one of the showiest and most attractive garden shrubs. The masses of small, bright yellow flowers are produced so thickly that the foliage is almost completely hidden. When not in bloom this is still a handsome shrub, with its oval, dark green leaves, compact habit of growth and small, pale flower buds, which contrast pleasantly with the foliage. The flower buds are noticeable from autumn and provide interest throughout the winter. Kumarahou seldom grows higher than two metres, although shaded or very sheltered specimens will sometimes be drawn up to a greater height. An open, sunny situation and a well-drained soil will produce the best display of flowers. Kumarahou plants flower from an early stage; those sold in nurseries usually flower the first season.

The only point against this colourful shrub is its tendency to be short lived. However, new plants are quickly established and it is easily raised from seed.

Pomaderris kumeraho

Seedlings often occur beneath the bushes and these are easily transplanted during winter, provided they are small. Kumarahou is liable to damage by anything more than moderate frosts, therefore where heavy frosts occur it should be grown in a warm, sheltered situation, such as against a north-facing wall.

Kumarahou grows naturally on poor clay soils around Auckland and further north. It is a common sight on the gumlands and is sometimes called gum-diggers' soap because the flower-heads will make a lather if rubbed between wet hands.

PRATIA
Lobeliaceae

There are five species of *Pratia* native to New Zealand. *P. angulata* is the best-known species in cultivation, although others such as *P. macrodon*, alpine panakenake, are also worthwhile. The natives should not be confused with the Australian species *P. pedunculata*, a mat-forming plant with masses of tiny, pale blue flowers, which is often grown in New Zealand gardens.

Pratia angulata
Panakenake, creeping pratia

A creeping, slender, mat-forming plant with small, soft leaves and shiny, white, star-shaped flowers. A charming hardy ground cover or rock-garden plant, which is very useful for creating a natural look with its informal, scrambling habit of growth. The flowers are produced in great numbers and often continue for several months, commencing in November. Purple-red berries ripen from late summer to autumn. Creeping pratia often lives up to its name, travelling from the garden into lawns and paths, but it is such a charming plant that this behaviour is easily forgiven, and its straying growths are simple to remove with a weeding knife or a fork. Its spread can also be halted by bushy, low-growing shrubs. A good, slightly moist soil is preferred and a sunny or lightly shaded situation is suitable.

Plants are easily propagated by cuttings or rooted layers. It can also be raised from seed.

PSEUDOPANAX
Araliaceae

The 15 species of *Pseudopanax* that occur in New Zealand are all endemic. They are shrubs or small trees, some of them very distinctive and pleasing in appearance. They are becoming increasingly popular for use in landscaping, particularly species such as *P. crassifolium* and *P. ferox*, which have a character all their own. Pseudopanax are noted for their ability to grow in virtually any soil, providing there is good drainage, and to stand up well to strong winds. Many are cold hardy but some, such as *P. lessonii* and its hybrids, *P.* 'Adiantifolium' and *P.* 'Gold Splash', need protection where frosts are heavy. *P. ferox* and *P. crassifolius* both have juvenile forms that are fascinating and highly ornamental.

Propagation of the species is by seed (which must be fresh) or by cuttings of firm tip growth. The hybrids and any distinct foliage forms must be propagated by cuttings.

Pseudopanax 'Adiantifolium'

This hybrid pseudopanax has striking foliage that resembles a giant maidenhair fern frond. It is a handsome, upright-growing shrub, which will attain a height of three metres or more. It is most distinctive in the garden, will grow in sun or shade and makes a good subject for a large container. It grows easily in any well-drained soil but will need a sheltered situation where heavy frosts are experienced.

Pratia angulata

Pseudopanax 'Adiantifolium'

Pseudopanax arboreus
Five-finger

A small, round-headed tree useful for shelter and for background planting. It has large, shiny, green leaves, which are divided into five to seven leaflets. The outline of a leaf resembles an outstretched hand. This handsome tree will grow in dry soils and stands up well to wind, although the foliage is larger and more attractive when it is growing in a good, moist soil. It is suitable for container growing.

Pseudopanax crassifolius
Lancewood, horoeka

The lancewood is a distinctive small tree, which is most effective for landscaping. A single tree makes a striking feature beside a building, while in a large garden or in public landscaping a group of trees is attractive. The lancewood has a distinct juvenile foliage stage during which the leaves are long and narrow, dark green and deeply toothed. As the years go by the foliage gradually becomes more rounded and shorter. It can take as long as 15 to 20 years before the adult form — a round-headed tree with dark foliage and a slender, greyish-coloured naked trunk — is assumed. The lancewood is hardy to cold and wind and will grow in virtually any soil providing there is reasonably good drainage.

Pseudopanax arboreus, five-finger

Pseudopanax crassifolius, lancewood

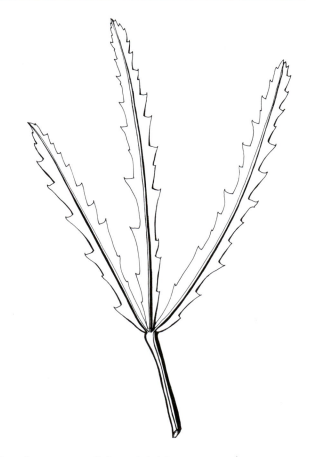

Pseudopanax crassifolius, adult foliage

Pseudopanax discolor

A large bushy shrub with light bronze-green leaves, divided into three to five leaflets in a similar manner to the leaves of *P. arboreus.* Not as striking as some other members of the genus but still a handsome shrub. Easy to grow. Cold hardy in most lowland districts.

Pseudopanax discolor 'Rangatira'

A striking cultivar that is similar to the species except for its dark bronze foliage. Provides a good colour contrast.

Pseudopanax ferox
Toothed lancewood

The juvenile foliage stage of this small tree is spectacular. During the first few years the leaves are long, narrow and very coarsely toothed. The colouring of these young leaves is also striking. They are a deep olive green with light-coloured, marbled markings and a prominent orange midrib. The toothed lancewood develops into a small tree with a straight and slender single trunk topped with a bushy head. The adult leaves are narrow and dark green. This little-known tree is ideal for small gardens, or anywhere that a most distinctive small tree is required. For bold landscaping effect, several trees can be grouped together, or one can be used as a dramatic focal point among low-growing shrubs or ornamental native grasses.

Pseudopanax 'Gold Splash'

The dark green leaves of *P.* 'Gold Splash' are boldly marked with golden yellow. This is one of the most striking foliage shrubs, either native or exotic, and offers many possibilities in landscaping. It forms a small tree, although it can be kept as a large shrub by means of a little pruning.

P. 'Gold Splash' is not as hardy to frost as most pseudopanax and where winters are severe it should be grown in a sheltered situation. It will grow in light shade just as satisfactorily as in the open and is sometimes seen as a striking feature tree growing against a south-facing house wall that the sun seldom reaches. This colourful native is also suitable for growing in a large container. It can remain in a half wine barrel for years if it is watered and fed regularly. At times the foliage reverts to plain green; if this occurs, cut out the plain green growths as soon as they are noticed.

Propagation is by cuttings of firm tip growth.

Pseudopanax ferox, juvenile leaf

Pseudopanax laetum

This is a striking shrub with bold shiny green foliage. It bears a resemblance to *P. arboreus* but is smaller and the leaves are much larger. *P. laetum* is a magnificent shrub for bold effect and should be used more often in landscaping. It combines superbly with native trees and shrubs of distinctive appearance such as flaxes, *Meryta sinclairii, Pseudopanax crassifolius,* tussock grasses and others. Despite its tropical appearance it is hardy in most districts; where frosts are heavy, the foliage may be damaged slightly if it is grown in the open, but this problem can be overcome by planting it in a sheltered position such as beneath tall trees.

P. laetum will grow to a height of approximately three metres and has a rounded, spreading habit. Any well-drained soil is suitable. It will tolerate dry conditions and poor soils but the foliage is biggest and most dramatic when this shrub is grown in a rich soil. It makes a handsome subject for a large container such as a half wine barrel.

Propagate by cuttings of firm tip growth or from seed.

Pseudopanax lessonii
Houpara

A handsome, bushy shrub with glossy green foliage. It stands up well to wind and grows easily in any well-drained soil but is not completely cold hardy; where frosts are heavy it must have protection. Combines well in a mixed shrub border. A good tub plant. *P. lessonii* hybridises readily with other pseudopanax species, notably *P. discolor,* and the resulting progeny are usually most attractive with widely varying and colourful foliage. Some beautiful purple-leaved forms have resulted from this cross.

PSEUDOWINTERA
Winteraceae

A genus of three endemic species. *P. colorata,* horopito or pepper tree, is of particular interest to gardeners for its colourful foliage. All the species will grow with ease in widely varying soils and are cold hardy.

They can be propagated by seed or cuttings.

Pseudopanax lessonii hybrids

Pseudopanax ferox, toothed lancewood

Pseudopanax 'Gold Splash'

Pseudowintera colorata
Horopito, pepper tree

A bushy, slow-growing shrub that seldom reaches a height of more than 1.5 metres under garden conditions. In the wild, however, it sometimes reaches the proportions of a small tree. The oblong foliage is a yellow-brown colour with red blotches, and when the brilliant red spring growth is present the effect is striking. This is a very worthwhile subject for gardens, making a pleasant change from some of the better-known foliage shrubs, which are so common that it is hard not to find them boring. Although it will tolerate quite poor conditions, it will grow better in a reasonably rich soil. Light soils can be improved by incorporating peat or compost before planting. *P. colorata* will grow in sun or shade, but bright light results in the best foliage colouring.

P. colorata is widespread in lowland forest throughout New Zealand.

The Maori name horopito and the common name pepper tree are applied to both *P. colorata* and *P. axillaris*. The leaves of both species are strongly aromatic when crushed, and bitter tasting. For the Maori and the early settlers, the leaves and bark of both provided valuable remedies for all sorts of ailments from toothache to gonorrhoea.

P. axillaris is similar in many ways to *P. colorata* but the leaves are dark green and lack the colourful markings. The third species, *P. traversii*, is a compact, slow-growing shrub with light green foliage. The eventual height is less than one metre. It is suitable for a rock garden or the foreground of a shrub border.

QUINTINIA
Escallioniaceae

There are three native species, all of which are endemic. *Q. acutifolia* is considered to be of most interest to gardeners. Plants are available from some nurseries specialising in native plants.

Quintinia acutifolia
Westland quintinia

A handsome, medium-sized tree with very attractive foliage. On young trees the leaves are yellow-green or bronze-green, often turning bronze during winter. Adult trees have light green foliage. During late spring and early summer narrow clusters of showy white flowers are produced near the tips of the branchlets. This little-known tree is attractive as a specimen and makes an interesting addition to a mixed group of trees and shrubs. It is hardy to cold and should have a reasonably rich soil. Watering during prolonged dry spells is recommended.

Despite the common name, *Q. acutifolia* is found in districts other than Westland, where it is especially plentiful. It also occurs on Great and Little Barrier Islands and from the Coromandel Peninsula to Waimarino and Taranaki.

Quintinia serrata
Tawheowheo

This tree is very similar to *Q. acutifolia* except for the leaves, which are narrower and often have blotchy markings. It occurs in the upper half of the North Island only.

RANUNCULUS
Ranunculaceae

Approximately 40 species of *Ranunculus* are native to New Zealand. Some are very beautiful but most are difficult to grow in lowland gardens, requiring cool conditions and a well-drained, moist soil. Shade from afternoon sun is necessary for success with most species. Plants are often difficult to obtain but they can sometimes be purchased from specialist alpine plant or native plant nurseries. For detailed information on growing some of the alpine species, Cartman's *Growing New Zealand Alpine Plants* is recommended.

Ranunculus lyallii
Great mountain buttercup, Mt Cook lily

This glorious plant has beautiful white buttercups on branching stems up to one metre high and large, round, deep green, glossy leaves. The flowering time is spring and summer. It occurs in high-rainfall areas of the mountains of the South Island. Its liking for lots of moisture and cool conditions makes it difficult

Ranunculus lyallii, great mountain buttercup

to accommodate in many gardens, but it can be grown in a cool, shady spot in soil that is rich in humus, well drained and does not dry out. It is one of only two white-flowered native *Ranunculus* species.

RAOULIA
Compositae

Approximately 20 species are native to New Zealand. Included in the genus are the fascinating, spectacular and notoriously difficult-to-grow 'vegetable sheep', which form great cushions of dense foliage in alpine regions. The mat-forming species, such as *R. australis* and *R. hookerii*, are considerably easier to grow and adapt well to cultivation providing they have excellent drainage and full sun. They must not be planted where there are overhanging branches that will cause drops of water to fall onto the foliage. A surface layer of gravel chips, or at the very least a gritty mixture of gravel and soil, is essential for success with these plants. They are ideal for rock gardens and look striking when carpeting the ground beneath a sharp-edged rock. Several different species growing together can make a fascinating pattern of varying textures and colours. On occasion raoulias die in patches. If this occurs, the dead growth should be cut away and the gap filled in with a combination of peat, sand and gravel. The bare area should soon be covered by new growth.

Raoulia australis
Scabweed

Forms dense, low mats of foliage, quickly covering an extensive area. Produces small yellow flowers prolifically in an open sunny situation. It is a variable

Raoulia hookerii

species but some good silver-foliage forms are in cultivation. *R.* 'Makara Form' has particularly attractive, tightly packed silver rosettes. Must have a very well-drained soil, preferably with a layer of fine gravel on the surface.

It is easy to propagate by division, cuttings or seed.

Raoulia haastii
Green mat daisy

Forms hard mats of tiny, moss-like foliage, which will cover a wide area. Grows with ease in a well-drained soil in full sun. The foliage varies in colour according to the season — bright green in spring, dark green in late summer, turning brown or bronze in winter. Established plants usually flower abundantly, becoming covered with tiny cream flowers in spring. A very attractive plant.

Raoulia hookeri
Common raoulia

Forms a thick mat of tiny, silver-green rosettes. It roots down as it spreads, soon forming a wide mat of silver. Should have full sun, well-drained conditions and a surface layer of gravel. A most appealing and easily grown plant, which is well suited to a rock garden.

Propagate by division or cuttings.

RHABDOTHAMNUS
Gesneriaceae

A genus consisting of a single species, which is widespread in lowland forests of the upper North Island and also occurs in localised areas as far south as Wellington. It is a delightful garden shrub for growing in shade.

Rhabdothamnus solandrii
Matata

A shade-loving, free-flowering, small shrub, which can grow as high as two metres but is often half this height. The oval leaves are medium green on their upper surfaces and silvery green on their undersides, with prominent veining. The leaf margins are toothed and both sides are covered with tiny, harsh hairs. The pale stems and a slender branching habit of growth add to the distinctive appearance of this shrub. The pretty bell-shaped flowers, which are produced over a long period, vary in colour from yellow to orange and red, and they often have darker red veining. Pruning encourages a bushier habit and a greater number of flowers.

R. solandrii prefers a well-drained soil rich in humus, but it will also grow in quite poor conditions. Light shade is ideal. It will tolerate only light frosts but can be grown where heavier frosts occur if positioned beneath a protective canopy of foliage.

The usual method of propagation is by semi-hardwood cuttings, although it can also be raised from seed. Taking cuttings is the only way of ensuring that a particular colour is perpetuated.

Rhabdothamnus solandrii

RHOPALOSTYLIS
Palmae

One of the most striking native plants, which could be used more frequently in gardens to provide a distinctive appearance. It is the only palm in the world to grow so far south in its wild state.

Rhopalostylis sapida
Nikau

This magnificent palm will grow as high as 10 metres, sometimes more, but takes many years to do so. A slow rate of growth seems to be the main reason why nikau is seldom encountered in gardens. In quite young plants the arching, feathery fronds are most attractive, and as a garden plant it has great potential for creating a bold, tropical look. As with many very upright trees of distinctive form, nikau looks most striking when planted in a group of three or more, although a solitary specimen is still most handsome. Nikau combines well with tree ferns or with pseudopanax, and can also be grown beneath tall trees providing the conditions are not too dry.

The pale purplish pink flowers are produced in large bunches at the base of the leaves, but it is usually 30 years or more before a nikau will start to flower. Flowers are followed by bright red fruits, which are popular with wood pigeons.

Nikau must have a reasonably sheltered situation. Only light frosts are tolerated and the soil should be rich and not allowed to dry out. It will grow in full sun or in shade.

Propagation is by seed.

RUBUS
Rosaceae

The five native species are all endemic. They are all scramblers or climbers and some have prickles, which can be a problem for the unwary. One species, *R. parvus*, is a creeper with distinctive foliage and is most attractive in the right situation.

Rubus parvus

A prostrate creeper that is useful as a ground cover, as a cascading plant for a wall or bank, and for crib walls. It is also of interest as a container plant. The long, narrow leaves are toothed and slightly prickly. They are an attractive bronze-green, the colour intensifying in cold weather. *R. parvus* looks particularly striking when the foliage is contrasted with ornamental rocks or stones. During late spring and early summer it has masses of small white flowers and these are followed by highly ornamental, bright red, raspberry-like fruits.

This plant grows readily in most soil types providing there is good drainage. However, the best displays of flowers and fruit and the brightest foliage colours occur when it is growing in a dry, sunny situation.

R. parvus grows in the wild from Nelson to south Westland, usually occurring on river banks and other stony areas.

Plants are easily propagated by seed or cuttings.

Rhopalostylis sapida, nikau palm

Rubus parvus

SCLERANTHUS
Caryophyllaceae

There are three species of *Scleranthus* native to New Zealand. They form rounded, moss-like cushions and are of interest for rock gardens, contrasting in texture with rocks and low plants. To grow well, they should have an open, sunny situation and a gritty, very free-draining soil. They are hardy to cold.

Can be propagated by cuttings or seed.

Scleranthus biflorus

Forms a loose mat of yellowish green. A lowland plant, it often grows on the coast, particularly in the North Island.

Scleranthus brockei

Has green foliage and forms a slightly tighter mat.

Scleranthus uniflorus

The most attractive species. Forms dense mats of yellow or orange foliage. It occurs throughout the South Island, up to a height of 1250 metres, and often grows in dry riverbeds and rocky places. Must have sharp drainage to succeed in cultivation.

SENECIO
Compositae

Some of the senecios native to New Zealand have recently been transferred to the genus *Brachyglottis*. Because the gardening public are so familiar with these plants under their old name of *Senecio*, it has been retained in this book.

Senecio greyii

A tough and very adaptable shrub with a spreading habit of growth, attractive grey foliage and bright yellow daisy flowers, which make a great show from early to mid-summer. It seldom reaches a height of more than 1.5 metres. *S. greyii* will grow in virtually any well-drained soil. It is cold hardy and can be grown in all districts, but it is in beach gardens that it is particularly useful for it withstands drought conditions and is unaffected by salt-laden sea winds. The only attention this shrub requires is a light trimming after flowering to keep it compact. Old bushes that have become straggly can be pruned severely and they will rapidly make new growth.

Propagation is by cuttings, which strike readily.

Senecio huntii
Rautini

This tall-growing species forms a large shrub or small tree. It is most distinctive, having numerous large heads of bright yellow flowers that are produced in mid-summer. The leaves are lance shaped, shiny green on the upper surface and greyish white beneath. *S. huntii* is native to the Chatham Islands, where it grows in peaty soils. In cultivation it grows well in an average to moderately rich soil and in a sunny situation. Plants should be watered thoroughly during dry weather, for this species is not tough and drought-resistant like *S. greyii*.

Senecio greyii

Senecio huntii

Solanum laciniatum, poroporo

SOLANUM
Solanaceae

Although the native *Solanum* species are generally regarded as little more than weeds, they are quite attractive in some situations. The two species are very similar and are both known by the common name poroporo.

Solanum aviculare
Solanum laciniatum
Poroporo

These two shrubs are very similar in many respects, but the flowers of *S. laciniatum* are larger and usually a brighter shade of purple-blue, with contrasting yellow stamens. The flower colour of *S. aviculare* varies from lavender to white. Both species have attractive orange-yellow berries, which, like the flowers, are produced over a long period. Birds, usually the bigger kinds from kakas to blackbirds, feed on the berries.

Both species are shrubs from 1.5 to three metres high, with a rounded, bushy habit. Quick growing and adaptable, they do well in light shade although plants in full sun produce more flowers. Soils that are well drained and rather poor are the most suitable. Poroporo will grow in rich soils but the growth tends to be rapid and lush in such conditions.

S. aviculare occurs in nature on the margins of coastal and lowland forests in the North Island and much of the upper half of the South Island as well as on the Chatham Islands, the Kermadecs and the Three Kings group. *S. laciniatum* occurs from about Auckland to Dunedin, being widespread in scrub country and on the verges of coastal and lowland forests.

Poroporo berries are poisonous when green. Both species are grown commercially for their berries, which contain a substance that is used to produce steroid hormones.

Propagation of poroporo is by seed, which germinates freely.

SOPHORA
Papilionaceae

Three species of *Sophora* are found in New Zealand; two are small trees and the third is usually a bushy or prostrate shrub. All three are known by the common name kowhai. Kowhai trees are widely regarded as being among the most outstanding flowering trees in the world. Anyone who has stood beneath a mature tree in full bloom on a sunny spring day and looked up at the pendulous yellow flowers against a background of blue sky will know why this is so. If the tree is full of boisterous, nectar-seeking native tuis, as blossoming kowhais so often are, then the scene is truly magic. The Maori people were also great admirers of these trees. The opening of the kowhai blooms was regarded as a sign that spring had arrived, and it is said that warm spring rains were often called 'kowhai rains'.

Kowhais have much to offer as garden trees. They grow readily in most soil types and are hardy to cold virtually anywhere in New Zealand. In exposed situations *S. microphylla* is regarded as the most suitable species to plant. As specimen trees kowhais are superb. Their handsome form is attractive throughout the year, and as a feature tree for a lawn or as a centrepiece for a paved sitting-out area, a kowhai is a first-rate choice. Kowhais are also superb for lining a driveway, as street trees, for planting in large groups to form a woodland and as background trees. Even *S. tetraptera*, the tallest species, is often suitable for small suburban gardens because of its open habit of growth and foliage that allows far more sunlight to penetrate than is the case with most other trees.

Where space is limited, *S. tetraptera* 'Gnome' should be planted, or one of the more compact varieties. Some interesting kowhai cultivars have been marketed lately and more should be available in future. One of the first named cultivars is 'Goldilocks',

Sophora tetraptera is suitable for planting as a street tree.

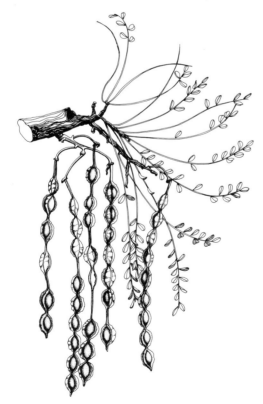
Sophora tetraptera seed-pods

which has golden-yellow flowers, blooms profusely and has an upright habit.

Kowhais are sometimes attacked by the kowhai moth, which feeds on the foliage and is capable of defoliating entire trees. This pest can be controlled by spraying with an insecticide such as carbaryl. Kowhais are seldom troubled by other pests or diseases.

Sophora microphylla
Kowhai

This kowhai, which occurs in the wild throughout New Zealand, on the Chatham Islands and in Chile, is distinguished from *S. tetraptera* by its smaller size (a maximum height of 10 metres), its slightly weeping habit and feathery foliage. Other differences include the colour of the flowers, usually bright yellow rather than the golden yellow of *S. tetraptera*, and the shape of the flowers, which are more squat and do not have the distinctive long keel of *S. tetraptera*. *S. microphylla* also has one other important characteristic that distinguishes it from *S. tetraptera*. Seedling trees undergo a juvenile stage during which they are twiggy bushes with lots of slender, wiry, intertwining, deep yellow branches. This stage persists for some years before the adult form is assumed. Vegetatively propagated plants, grown from cuttings taken from mature trees, do not undergo this stage.

There are two varieties of *S. microphylla*. Variety *fulvida* grows in coastal scrub and forest west of Auckland, flowering in October or November. It has small leaves, large lemon-yellow flowers, a compact habit of growth and does not undergo a juvenile stage. All these points make it a good candidate for planting in gardens, but it is seldom offered for sale, even by specialist native plant nurseries.

S. microphylla variety *longicarinata* (formerly *S. treadwellii*) is a small, slender tree with small leaves and pale yellow flowers larger than those of *S. microphylla*. Mature trees seldom attain a height greater than 3.5 metres, and its dimensions make it a good choice for small gardens. It comes from Takaka in the South Island.

Sophora prostrata
Prostrate kowhai

The prostrate kowhai is really a plant for the collector of the unusual for it lacks the attributes that make for a worthwhile garden plant. Under garden conditions it forms a tangled mass of growth one to two metres high, and its habit of flowering sparsely is not likely to find favour with most gardeners.

Sophora tetraptera
Kowhai

S. tetraptera, the North Island kowhai, is the most popular species in cultivation and is a common sight

Sophora tetraptera, kowhai

Sophora tetraptera 'Gnome'

in gardens throughout New Zealand. It seldom grows higher than 12 metres, forming a spreading tree that is handsome throughout the year. The golden yellow flowers are produced in spring, the exact time varying from August to September or October, according to locality and the genetic make-up of individual trees. *S. tetraptera* is hardy in most areas of New Zealand and should be planted more often as a specimen tree.

Sophora tetraptera 'Gnome'

A slow-growing dwarf cultivar, which in time forms a rounded shrub about two metres high. It has the largest flowers of any kowhai, and an established shrub in full bloom is outstanding. The usual flowering time is September or October. *S. tetraptera* 'Gnome' combines well with spring-flowering hebes with blue or mauve-blue flowers, such as the prostrate-growing *Hebe* 'Hartii', and with bronze-foliaged tussock grasses such as *Carex lucida*. For a dazzling combination, plant this kowhai near the shrubby or climbing form of *Metrosideros carminea*, which has brilliant red flowers at the same time. One drawback of *S. tetraptera* 'Gnome' is its rather stiff habit of growth, but this can be minimised by careful positioning in the garden. This is a natural choice of kowhai for small gardens.

It breeds true to type from seed and can also be propagated by cuttings.

TECOMANTHE
Bignoniaceae

Tecomanthe speciosa is one of the rarest of native plants in the wild. Only one plant was ever discovered, on Great Island of the Three Kings group. Thankfully, the preservation of this plant is assured by its popularity with gardeners and it is now well established in cultivation.

Tecomanthe speciosa

A rapid-growing, sometimes rampant climber of interest for its ornamental foliage as well as its flowers. Left to its own devices, this vine is likely to cover a considerable area, twining around or through anything that offers support, be it verandah posts or trees. It is easily controlled by a little pruning and makes a delightful covering for a wall or to drape over an archway or pergola.

T. speciosa is frost tender, and anything more than a light frost will cause damage. However, it can be grown in areas with quite cold winters if provided

Tecomanthe speciosa

Tecomanthe speciosa foliage

with a protected, warm situation, such as a north-facing house wall with overhead shelter provided by the eaves. It will flower well in sun or light shade. Flowering time is usually from late autumn to early winter, although well-established vines will sometimes bloom over a longer period. The pale, creamy-yellow flowers are striking, up to seven centimetres long, tube shaped with a flared mouth. They are produced from the old wood, hanging in bunches, and are marvellous when viewed from below, making the vine a good choice for pergolas. The native tui delight in the flowers, especially as they occur at a time when food is often scarce for nectar-eating birds. Tecomanthe foliage is shiny green and smooth, each leaf consisting of several pairs of oval leaflets and a large end leaflet.

Propagation is relatively easy, by either seed or cuttings. The latter method produces plants that flower at an earlier stage. Even so, plants are unlikely to bloom for a few years after planting.

UNCINIA
Cyperaceae

There are approximately 32 native *Uncinia* species. These sedges all have hooked seed-heads, which attach themselves to passers-by. Most are of little interest horticulturally, but one alpine species, *U. rubra*, is an attractive garden plant.

Uncinia rubra

A dwarf (30 centimetres), tufted grass with reddish foliage, *U. rubra* looks striking when combined with low ground covers such as *Acaena* species. It also looks good growing alongside native tussock grasses and makes a delightful contrast with small shrubs such as some of the dwarf hebes. *U. rubra* is interesting grown beside a small pool, or among pebbles or small

Uncinia rubra

rocks. In the wild the foliage colour varies from reddish green to dark coppery red. The darkest colour forms are usually offered for sale. Although the natural habitat of this plant is often damp, peaty grassland, it seems perfectly happy in any average garden soil providing it is not too dry. Full sun brings out the best foliage colour.

Propagation of good colour forms is usually by division of clumps; each rooted piece will grow. Seedlings are likely to vary in foliage colour.

VIOLA
Violaceae

There are three native *Viola* species. They usually grow in damp, shaded places in the wild. In gardens they grow well in a moist, shaded portion of a rock garden, combining well with dwarf ferns and low-growing plants such as *Pratia angulata* and *Mazus* species.

Viola cunninghamii

This is the most desirable species and the most readily available. It has deep green leaves, a tufted habit, and white flowers with mauve markings. The flowering time is October to January. It is easy to grow providing it has a damp soil.

VITEX
Verbenaceae

The magnificent puriri is the only representative of the genus *Vitex* that occurs naturally in New Zealand. It is one of the finest of all native trees.

Vitex lucens, puriri

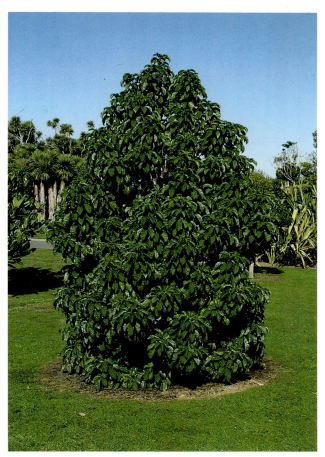

Vitex lucens — a young tree

Vitex lucens
Puriri

As a tall specimen tree for gardens, puriri is outstanding but its size (up to 20 metres) makes it unsuitable for smaller areas. It forms a massive tree when fully grown, with a great dome-shaped canopy of shiny green foliage and a stout trunk. Puriri trees should be planted where they have room to spread and their form can be appreciated, rather than crowded in among other trees. A solitary specimen in a farm paddock or on a large lawn can be striking, and a puriri woodland is magnificent. It is a worthwhile street tree, although care must be taken not to position trees beneath overhead wires or they will become a problem in time. In rich, deep soil, ideal for puriri, the initial rate of growth tends to be rapid.

Puriri is susceptible to frost. Young trees are particularly tender and are liable to suffer damage from just a few degrees of frost, but established specimens will withstand light to moderate frosts. This tenderness is reflected in the natural distribution of puriri; it is by nature a tree of warmer regions, growing near the coast, in lower hill forests of the Far North and in localised areas as far south as Poverty Bay on the east coast and Taranaki to the west.

The foliage of puriri is notable for its leathery feel and the way the bold leaflets are arranged in a finger-like pattern. The attractive flowers are a dull pinkish red, usually occurring in greatest numbers in spring, although the flowering period extends for much of the year. The fruits of puriri are up to two centimetres across and hang in clusters like overly large, bright red cherries when ripe. A tree laden with fruit is an impressive sight.

The heaviest crops of fruit tend to be in late summer, but as with the flowers, some fruit can usually be found on the tree throughout the year. Both flowers and fruit attract native birds, especially tuis and wood pigeons.

The wood of puriri is strong and durable but is sometimes spoilt by the larvae of the puriri moth. An uneven and irregular grain makes the wood difficult to work. In the past puriri wood was used for house blocks, railway sleepers and wharf piles.

Puriri seed germinates freely. Young seedlings often occur beneath established trees and these will transplant if lifted with care during the winter months. Cuttings will strike, but this is not the usual method of propagation.

WAHLENBERGIA
Campanulaceae

There are approximately 10 species of *Wahlenbergia* native to New Zealand. They are small, hardy plants suitable for growing in rock gardens. Some are insignificant, even weedy, but the best species are delightful, with compact, tidy, green foliage and blue or white bluebell-like flowers on long dainty stems for weeks on end in summer. A sunny situation and excellent drainage are needed to grow these plants

well. A mulch of stone chips around the plants will help to provide natural growing conditions and prevents the foliage becoming splashed with soil.

Plants can be propagated by severing rooted rhizomes, by cuttings or seed.

Wahlenbergia albomarginata

One of the most attractive species, it has large flowers, as much as three centimetres across, on slender stems. The flower colour varies from white through various shades of blue. It is one of the easiest species to grow and will sometimes produce a few flowers at odd times throughout the year as well as in summer. Tends to spread, but is easily controlled.

Wahlenbergia brockei

Easy to grow providing it has sharp drainage. The flowers are pale blue, produced individually on slender stems.

Wahlenbergia matthewsii

A very attractive, bushy, strong-growing but sometimes short-lived plant. The flowers are as large as those of *W. albomarginata*, on tall stems, and vary in colour from white to pale blue.

WEINMANNIA
Cunoniaceae

Two species of *Weinmannia* occur in New Zealand and both are attractive trees. *W. racemosa*, kamahi, is of the most interest for garden use.

Weinmannia racemosa
Kamahi

Kamahi will eventually develop into a tall tree but it remains compact for many years and can be kept as a shrub by regular clipping. During the winter the foliage of immature trees takes on bright reddish brown to red colourings. As well as being very ornamental in the garden, the winter foliage is popular for floral work. The foliage of adult trees is dark green all year round. Kamahi blooms profusely in early to late summer. The racemes of creamy white flowers resemble those of some hebes and a specimen in full bloom is most attractive.

Kamahi deserves to be grown more in gardens. Most soil types are suitable and it will grow virtually anywhere except in exposed beach gardens. It can be used for shelter and is occasionally seen as a hedge. Kamahi is cold hardy.

It occurs over much of the country in lowland and mountain forests.

Propagation is by seed or cuttings.

Vitex lucens — mature tree in a New Plymouth street

Weinmannia racemosa, kamahi

Xeronema callistemon, Poor Knight's lily

Weinmannia silvicola
Tawhero, towai

This species can be distinguished from kamahi by its foliage; the juvenile leaves have up to five pairs of leaflets and the adult foliage consists of three leaflets. The green leaves do not take on the colourful tints of kamahi.

W. silvicola flowers profusely, the entire tree becoming a mass of creamy blooms in summer. It forms an upright tree, often reaching a height of 15 metres. Although it is attractive, it is arguably less ornamental than kamahi, but it deserves to be included in any collection of native trees. Its natural distribution is restricted to the upper North Island, but it is hardy in most districts. Most soil types are suitable and it will grow in shade or in the open.

Propagate by seed or cuttings.

XERONEMA
Agavaceae

One species occurs in New Zealand, found on the Poor Knights and Hen and Chickens islands off the north-eastern coast. It is a spectacular plant, which grows well in gardens where the climate is mild.

Xeronema callistemon
Poor Knights lily, raupo-taranga

Xeronema (pronounced 'Zeronema') *callistemon* forms large clumps of shiny, light green, sword-like, erect foliage up to 75 centimetres high. Sharp drainage, full sun and protection from frost are required for successful culture. It is suitable for growing in a rock garden; the cool root run provided by surrounding rocks seems to suit it well. This unusual plant is also suitable for growing in containers providing the potting medium is free draining. During long, hot spells an occasional watering is desirable.

Xeronema callistemon takes some years to reach flowering stage, but anyone who has seen a plant in full bloom would agree that it is worth waiting for. The extraordinary flowers are like giant tooth-brushes with fat, scarlet bristles. The flowers arise from the centre of the clump, arching out as they develop so the flowers point upwards. Well-established clumps can produce as many as 25 of the spectacular flower-stems. Flowering time is late spring, usually about November.

Plants are usually propagated from seed, which germinates readily when fresh. Established clumps can also be divided.

FERNS

FERNS

There are more than 150 species of ferns in New Zealand. Many require special conditions that are hard to duplicate, but there are still significant numbers that adapt well to garden conditions and thrive with a minimum of attention.

Ferns provide the garden with a special character, for they are unique among plants and the most attractive species are beautiful. Ferns are superb for growing in situations such as along the south-facing wall of a house or on a moist, shady bank, where comparatively few plants will grow satisfactorily. They can be used as ground covers, planted *en masse* beneath trees, or small species can be used to edge a shady path or as a foil to flowering plants.

Native ferns do not have to be grown exclusively with other natives. They combine well with exotic plants ranging from annuals to shrubs and trees. Ferns chosen for their graceful fronds and the free-flowering and brightly coloured impatiens, grown together in a shady spot, will make a charming combination for summer. Tree ferns are magnificent as a backdrop to colourful shrubs, as anyone who has visited the Pukeiti rhododendron grounds on the slopes of Mount Egmont will be well aware. In a bog garden, tree ferns make a dramatic contrast to colourful, moisture-loving perennials such as primulas, irises and hostas.

Most ferns require shelter from strong wind and draughts if they are to grow well. Shade is also important for the majority of ferns, although there are some that will grow in sun. The delightful *Doodia media* is an example of one of the more adaptable species that thrive in either sun or shade.

The ideal soil for most ferns is one that is rich in humus. Light soils should have a good quantity of organic matter such as compost, leaf mould or peat incorporated prior to planting. Although ferns like moist soil, most need good drainage to grow well. Heavy clays can be made more suitable by mixing in sand and organic matter.

In dry weather ferns should be watered thoroughly at regular intervals. This is particularly important when they are grown beneath large trees where the ground often becomes very dry.

If using fertiliser, it pays to be cautious. Large amounts of fertilisers high in nitrogen may harm ferns. A little blood and bone or well-decayed animal manure (cow is excellent) will prove sufficient. Do not lime around ferns; they like an acid soil, and lime is likely to set them back rather than boost their growth.

GROWING FERNS FROM SPORES

Ferns do not produce flowers or seed. Sexual reproduction of ferns is accomplished by means of the minute spores that develop on the undersides of the fronds. A good way of gathering fern spores is to cut off a small piece of fertile frond and place it, spore side down, between two sheets of paper in a warm position. It should take only a few days for the spores to drop onto the paper.

The spores are now ready for sowing, but they must be handled carefully for they are as fine as dust. Tip the spores into a dry container such as an envelope. They should be sown promptly; the longer the spores are kept, the less chance there is of them germinating for they remain fertile for a brief period only.

The medium used to raise the fern spores should be sterilised if possible. This can be achieved simply by pouring boiling water over the seed raising compost. Take care to allow the compost to cool off properly before sowing the spores. A popular mixture for the seed compost is 75 per cent peat moss and 25 per cent river sand. Another method of raising fern spores, which is highly successful, is to sow them straight onto a clay building brick that is kept moist. The spores should be scattered thinly.

Whatever method is used to raise fern spores, they must be kept moist. Good light, but never direct sunlight, is ideal. Covering the spores with plastic or a sheet of glass supported above the growing medium will reduce moisture loss considerably. This covering should remain until the ferns reach the true frond stage, by which time they are ready for potting up.

NATIVE FERNS FOR GARDENS

Asplenium bulbiferum
Hen and Chickens fern, manamana

A beautiful fern with long, recurving fronds. It grows to a height of about 50 centimetres, sometimes more. This species is comparatively easy to grow and looks delightful when used in a large group beneath trees. It is very easy to increase, for small ferns form on the tips of the fronds and these can be detached and potted up before planting out.

Asplenium hookerianum

A dainty fern with small, dull green fronds up to 20 centimetres long. It is easy to grow and will tolerate dry conditions once established. Slugs and snails seem to have a liking for the fronds, but slug bait will prevent problems.

Blechnum capense

One of the most adaptable ferns, capable of growing in sun or shade. It is ideal for covering difficult banks and in the wild is often seen colonising road cuttings. In good conditions the fronds are large, sometimes measuring more than a metre long, but in less favourable situations the fronds may be less than half this length. It is cold hardy.

Blechnum discolor
Crown fern, piupiu

This fern forms crowns of semi-upright fronds on short trunks. It is a large and handsome fern, which grows well if provided with a cool, shaded spot in the garden. If there is room, plant several together for a bold effect.

Blechnum filiforme
Thread fern

A most unusual fern with two distinct foliage forms. While growing on the ground the fronds are always small and finely divided, but whenever it climbs up a tree the fronds above ground level are much larger. Likes shade and a sheltered spot.

Can be propagated by simply lifting and replanting a piece of rooted rhizome.

Blechnum penna-marina
Small hardfern

A pretty little creeping fern, which is very easy to grow. It will quickly cover a small area and is a good ground cover or rock-garden plant. The new fronds are a reddish colour. Will grow in sun or light shade with equal ease but is not so happy in dense shade.

One of the easiest of ferns to propagate; any rooted piece will grow.

Doodia media

A most rewarding small fern with slender, upright fronds, this species grows well with a minimum of attention. It is perfectly happy in sun or light shade and is able to withstand dry conditions without ill effect. The new fronds are a striking rosy-red and in the spring it is an attractive sight. In time *D. media* forms quite a patch.

Hypolepsis tenuifolia

This creeping fern with dull green fronds is a useful ground cover for shady spots. It will spread over quite a distance, a useful characteristic where there is a large area to cover, but in small gardens other creeping ferns are likely to prove more satisfactory.

Lastreopsis hispida

A charming fern for moist soil and shaded conditions. The deep green fronds are long and broad and most attractive. It grows easily and spreads to form quite a clump in the garden. *L. hispida* can also be grown in baskets, providing it is kept moist. The fronds can be dried and used in floral arrangements.

Marattia salicina
King fern, para

One of the most beautiful native ferns. Its big, luxuriant, shiny, green fronds can measure anything from 1.8 to three metres or more in length and one metre or more across. This striking fern has a tropical look to it, and providing it has a moist, rich soil and protection from frost, it will grow well. The king fern can be grown as a pot plant indoors while young, but it usually becomes too large for a container after a few years.

Plants can be propagated by carefully removing the horseshoe-like appendages with a leaf bud attached from the base of the plant.

Asplenium bulbiferum, hen and chickens fern

Phymatosorus diversifolius
Hound's tongue

An attractive and distinctive fern with tongue-shaped, shiny, bright green fronds. It will cover quite an area on the ground as well as climbing any handy tree trunks. Grows with ease in all sorts of conditions but is happiest in damp shade.

Can be propagated by severing rhizomes.

Phymatosorus scandens

This species is similar to *P. diversifolius* but the fronds are more slender and it needs something to climb over; it will not grow on the ground. It is a useful and most attractive fern for covering an old stump or for growing on rocks. Moist shade is required.

Polystichum richardii
Shield fern

The stiff fronds of this fern are held erect and have a harsh texture that makes them almost prickly to the touch. It forms tufts of dark green fronds up to 75 centimetres high. The shield fern grows easily in a variety of situations. Once established, it tolerates sun and will also withstand a reasonable amount of wind and drought.

Polystichum vestitum
Prickly shield fern

A lovely fern with dark, rather dull green fronds, which are up to 90 centimetres long and are harsh to the touch. It is hardy and grows with ease providing it has a good moist soil that contains plenty of humus. Position it in shade or where it receives sun in the morning only.

Pteris macilenta

A lovely fern with soft, lacy, pale green fronds. The fronds can measure anything from 30 to 90 centimetres in length. It grows well in a cool, damp spot in soil containing plenty of humus.

TREE FERNS

Cyathea dealbata
Ponga, silver fern

The fronds of this well-known and easily recognised tree fern have silvery undersides. It is a tall-growing species but its rate of growth is comparatively slow, making it suitable for small gardens. This beautiful fern is easy to grow providing it is sheltered from wind. Once established, the silver fern will tolerate quite dry conditions and it is hardy to cold.

Cyathea medullaris

Cyathea medullaris
Mamaku

Mamaku is the tallest native tree fern, a majestic beauty that forms a black trunk 15 to 20 metres high topped by a crown of big, drooping, dark green fronds. It is marvellous for providing a dramatic, tropical look but its size precludes it from most small gardens. A sheltered situation is ideal but it will stand up to a reasonable amount of wind. The fronds may be damaged by severe frosts but there should be few problems with cold in most lowland districts. During extended periods of dry weather, plants should be watered thoroughly. Mamaku is a comparatively rapid grower.

Cyathea smithii
Whe

This handsome tree fern is hardy to cold but the fronds are easily damaged by wind, therefore it should have a sheltered situation such as beneath tall trees. A moist soil is required. Its large fronds are bright green and soft in texture.

Dicksonia fibrosa
Wheki-ponga

A handsome species with a stout trunk and medium green fronds, which are more ascending than other native tree ferns. It grows slowly and can be accommodated in small gardens without much difficulty. The old fronds remain on the tree for a long time in nature, but in the garden they can be cut off as they turn brown. Wheki-ponga is very hardy to cold, and the fronds are tough and not easily damaged by wind.

Dicksonia fibrosa

Dicksonia squarrosa
Wheki

An attractive and very hardy, medium-sized tree fern. It has a slender trunk and harsh, medium green fronds. The old fronds persist long after they have turned brown. The fronds stand up well to sun and wind, but it is preferable for the roots to be in shade. Wheki looks delightful when several are planted in a clump. One of the most adaptable species, it will grow in any reasonable soil providing it is not too dry.

BIBLIOGRAPHY

Burstall, S. W. and Sale, E. V. (1984) *Great Trees of New Zealand*

Cartman, Joe. (1985) *Growing New Zealand Alpine Plants*

Eagle, Audrey. (1982) *Eagle's Trees and Shrubs of New Zealand*. Second series

Fisher, Muriel E. (1984) *Gardening with New Zealand Ferns*

Fisher, Muriel E., Satchell, E., Watkins, Janet M. (1970) *Gardening with New Zealand Plants, Shrubs and Trees*

Moore, L. B. and Edgar, E. (1970) *Flora of New Zealand: Volume 2*

Harrison, Richmond E. (1974) *Handbook of Trees and Shrubs*

Macdonald, Christina. (1974) *Medicines of the Maori*

Mark, A. F. and Adams, Nancy M. (1979) *New Zealand Alpine Plants*

Matthews, Barbara. (1979) *Growing Native Plants*

Matthews, Julian. (1983) *AA Trees in New Zealand*

Metcalf, L. J. (1972) *The Cultivation of New Zealand Trees and Shrubs*

Moore, L. B. and Irwin, J. B. (1978) *The Oxford Book of New Zealand Plants*

Salmon, J. T. (1980) *The Native Trees of New Zealand*

INDEX

Julian Matthews is a horticultural journalist who is well known for his books and magazine and newspaper articles on gardening. Through his writing he encourages people to make better use of New Zealand plants, many of which he feels are more interesting and better suited to local conditions than the widely planted exotics.

He is also a keen photographer and takes all his own photographs to illustrate his books and articles, as well as photographs for other authors' work.

Julian is currently editor of *New Zealand Gardener* and the gardening columnist for *North and South* magazine. He is also the author of *A.A. Trees in New Zealand, Creative Home Landscaping in New Zealand, The New Zealander's Garden, The New Zealand Garden Book* and *Landscaping Ideas for New Zealand Gardens.*

When he is not travelling around New Zealand gathering information and photographs for his books and articles, Julian lives on the Kapiti Coast north of Wellington with his journalist wife, Liz.